The
Essential
Marcus
Aurelius

THE TARCHER CORNERSTONE EDITIONS

Tao Te Ching
by Lao Tzu, translated by Jonathan Star

The Essential Marcus Aurelius
newly translated and introduced
by Jacob Needleman and John P. Piazza

Accept This Gift: Selections from A Course in Miracles
edited by Frances Vaughan, Ph.D., and Roger Walsh, M.D., Ph.D.
foreword by Marianne Williamson

The Kybalion
by Three Initiates

The Spiritual Emerson
Essential Works by Ralph Waldo Emerson
introduction by Jacob Needleman

JEREMY P. TARCHER/PENGUIN
a member of Penguin Group (USA) Inc.
New York

The
Essential
Marcus
Aurelius

Newly translated and introduced by

JACOB NEEDLEMAN

and JOHN P. PIAZZA

JEREMY P. TARCHER/PENGUIN
Published by the Penguin Group
Penguin Group (USA) Inc., 375 Hudson Street, New York, New York 10014, USA •
Penguin Group (Canada), 90 Eglinton Avenue East, Suite 700, Toronto, Ontario M4P 2Y3,
Canada (a division of Pearson Canada Inc.) • Penguin Books Ltd, 80 Strand,
London WC2R 0RL, England • Penguin Ireland, 25 St Stephen's Green, Dublin 2, Ireland
(a division of Penguin Books Ltd) • Penguin Group (Australia), 250 Camberwell Road,
Camberwell, Victoria 3124, Australia (a division of Pearson Australia Group Pty Ltd) •
Penguin Books India Pvt Ltd, 11 Community Centre, Panchsheel Park, New Delhi–110 017,
India • Penguin Group (NZ), 67 Apollo Drive, Rosedale, North Shore 0632,
New Zealand (a division of Pearson New Zealand Ltd) • Penguin Books (South Africa)
(Pty) Ltd, 24 Sturdee Avenue, Rosebank, Johannesburg 2196, South Africa

Penguin Books Ltd, Registered Offices: 80 Strand, London WC2R 0RL, England

Most Tarcher/Penguin books are available at special quantity discounts for bulk purchase for
sales promotions, premiums, fund-raising, and educational needs. Special books or book ex-
cerpts also can be created to fit specific needs. For details, write Penguin Group (USA) Inc.
Special Markets, 375 Hudson Street, New York, NY 10014.

Library of Congress Cataloging-in-Publication Data

Marcus Aurelius, Emperor of Rome, 121–180.
[Meditations. English. Selections]
The essential Marcus Aurelius / newly translated and introduced by Jacob Needleman
and John P. Piazza.
p.   cm.
Includes bibliographical references and index.
ISBN 978-1-58542-617-1 (alk. paper)
1. Ethics.   2. Stoics.   3. Life.   I. Needleman, Jacob.   II. Piazza, John P.   III. Title.
B581.N44   2008   2007046041
188—dc22

Printed in the United States of America
25th Printing

BOOK DESIGN BY NICOLE LAROCHE

Contents

Introduction

JACOB NEEDLEMAN

What could be clearer? No other life is more appropriate for the practice of philosophy than that which you now happen to be living.

MEDITATIONS, II.7

What is the secret of this remarkable book? What has enabled it now and in the past to speak to countless men and women throughout the world without evoking anything but quiet respect and gratitude? We know that the works of the great philosophers—from Plato and Aristotle to the modern giants Nietzsche, Heidegger, and Wittgenstein—all have their passionate, sometimes angry, defenders and detractors. Not so this profoundly influential book. Although there are scholarly disagreements about the meaning of certain passages, hardly a trace of agitation or feverish controversy has ever found its way into the atmosphere of this text. Why is that? What enables these private, intimate meditations of the emperor of Rome to transcend the noise of his (and our) embattled world? What enables his words to reach so gently across the millennia, offering us the hope and the taste of an inner strength that only a quiet mind can bring?

Simply to summarize the main ideas in the book can give no sense of the power it has to help people face the vicissitudes that are the lot of every human life—the shocks, the terrors, the disappointments, the sorrows, as well as the overmastering "triumphs" and cravings that sweep us away; the betrayals that wound and confound us; and the specter of death that shadows every moment of the days and years that are given us to live on earth. Yes, the book offers us the great idea of the Mind of the universe calling to us from within our own mind. And, yes, it speaks of the inner freedom that we experience when we step back in ourselves and try to listen to that call. The cultivation of this inner freedom, says Marcus, is both our deepest human possibility and the real root of the self-respect and moral power for which we yearn—the ability to love and act justly in the conduct of our lives.

Such ideas help us not to give up. They inspire us and bring honorable, realistic hope in our own embattled lives. And this hope Marcus offers us with an unsurpassed blending of metaphysical vision, poetic genius, and the worldly realism of a ruler whose realm comprises nearly half the peoples of the known world. For this alone, this book deserves its unique place among the writings of the world's great spiritual philosophers.

But this in itself does not represent the real secret of this book and its action upon us. It is not the ideas alone that reach into us with such compassionate precision; nor is it simply the subtlety and economy with which they are expressed.

No, to discover the real secret of this book, you must open it when life is breaking your heart or when you are engulfed by anxiety or self-pity or resentment or—far more difficult—open it when all your dreams seem to be coming true and it seems that all will be well forever. What is it about the book that mercifully brings us to a stop—in the form of a completely new sense of inner dignity and strength? Not the strength that promises victory over our enemies, or that promises the pleasures of money, food, or sex, or even health and freedom from pain. And not the "dignity" of self-importance that comes from the praise of others or from the many and varied badges of honor which the world persuades us to take so seriously. And not even from our ability to withstand difficulty and hardship without flinching, although that may certainly be a great virtue in its own proper place.

Again, no. The secret of this book does not lie in such things, though it is often interpreted in that way.

The real secret of the book lies in the fact that Marcus is writing these meditations to himself and to himself alone— not to you or me or to any of the many thousands of us who, over the centuries, have carried this book with them. He is writing to *himself.* He is expressing to *himself* what he is trying and inwardly questioning through his own awakened attention in the present moment.

Few of us, of course, can have any idea what his inner state must be like as he reflects and writes; nor of the immensity of the forces that are combining upon him and within him—Marcus Aurelius, emperor of Rome, carrying nearly the world itself on his shoulders, determining the life and death of millions, judging, ruling, killing and rescuing; the emperor of Rome, marooned in the swamps of Eastern Europe with the great Roman army defending the Empire against "barbarian hordes," the likes of which are eventually destined to bring down the Empire of a Thousand Years; the emperor of Rome, poor human being that he is, target of both adoration and murderous hatred, a man suffering and dying from an unknown illness as he sits late and alone in his tent. Under the force of such inner and outer conditions, his words reflect the uniquely human work of attending consciously to one's own mind, one's own developing soul. It is this pure inner search for self-knowledge under the most harrowing of conditions that brings such penetrating practical intelligence to the philosophical ideas he has studied throughout his life, charging his vision of the universe and God and the conduct of life with such a contagious, compassionate objectivity toward himself and the forces of life. The pages of this book are, in fact, a testament to the transforming effect that the awakening of conscious attention has upon the workings of the human mind and heart.

Is it this, then—this effect upon himself, not so much of the great universal ideas he turns to but of his inner questioning as such—is *this* the secret of the *Meditations* of Marcus Aurelius?

Yes, but we must look still further.

I suggest that there is yet another secret in these writings, *a secret within the secret.* I believe we can detect something in this book that is quite rare in philosophical writing, at least in most modern philosophical texts. It seems clear to me that as he is writing, Marcus is often intensely and carefully watching his own thoughts and impulses with a sincerity and power of attention that is much more difficult to attain than we may imagine. That, as I say, is part of the secret of this book. But the secret within the secret lies in the fact that such self-expression of the inner search at the same time awakens and guides the attention of the reader to his or her own thoughts and impulses. And just as, in these instances, Marcus is seeking to *experience* from within himself the higher attention of what he calls the *logos,* or Universal Reason, so too the sensitive reader begins to listen for that same finer life within his own psyche. That is to say, the reader—you and I—is not simply given great ideas which he then feeds into his already formed opinions and rules of logic. The action of many of these meditations is far more serious than that, and far more interesting and spiritually practical. In a word, in such cases, in many of these meditations, we are being *guided*—without even necessarily knowing what to call it—we are being guided through a brief moment of inner work. We are being given a taste of what it means to step back in ourselves and develop an *intentional relationship to our own mind*.

And what Marcus would have us (and himself) understand—and here is the great power of these writings—is that this is the source of true self-respect in human life. Marcus is telling us, and in a certain definite sense he is *showing us* (think again of the conditions under which he is writing!) that no matter what befalls us, no matter what life deals us, no matter what temptations or suffering we encounter, no matter how shaken we are or bored or torn by impossible demands and choices, no matter what is happening to us in the life we happen to be living, it is always possible for us to step back within ourselves and rediscover an intentional relationship to our own mind (which includes our thoughts, emotions, and sensations). No one and nothing can take that possibility from us. I am a human being. I am not, first and foremost, a man or a woman, not an animal, not a computer, not a car, not a bank account, not a professor, senator, soldier, not even a mother or father. I am first and foremost a human being, and it is of the essence of a human being that he has the possibility (and, as Marcus will tell us, the high duty) to cultivate the capacity to step back from himself and become conscious of himself—the capacity and the responsibility to remember what he is as both an individual personality living just here and now, in this or that circumstance, and as a human being who has within himself (who *is* within oneself) a conscious particle of divinity.

But there is yet more. Throughout the meditations, while Marcus is communicating his struggle not to attach himself to his emotional judgments and thought associations, he speaks of the fundamental wish to open himself to the Mind of the Whole, what we often translate here as "Reason." It is clear that he is not speaking only of a comforting, interesting philosophical idea which may bring consolation or may, therapeutically, take our mind away from troubling or agitating thoughts. He is not speaking of a mere idea or concept. He is speaking of a palpable force that has material effects on his thinking, his feeling, and his action in the world. To be more precise, he is speaking of his struggle to open himself to an identity—a self within himself—that has the capacity to obey and transmit the Mind of the Whole into the bones and muscles of his own human body. Does he succeed in effecting this opening? Perhaps, perhaps not, in this or that case. But the reader can sense Marcus' need for that opening, and his certainty that it is not only possible but necessary—indeed, that it is the most necessary work that a human being can undertake, for it is through such contact with the principle of Mind within oneself that an individual is given the true capacity to live fully and vibrantly the life he has been given, and to act justly toward one's fellow man.

And the reader finds himself not only thinking about the

idea of the "ruling principle" in oneself, which directly obeys and transmits the Mind of the Whole, but may actually find him- or herself waiting inwardly, searching inwardly for that contact, that relation to one's own higher attention. It is in this silent inner waiting, however momentary, that the reader finds the unique power of this remarkable book. Even as its ideas place our lives in a broader cosmic perspective (one of the central roles of real philosophy), at the same time the beginning of a profound psychological, metaphysical process occurs within us that deepens and quiets our ordinary sense of self. For a fleeting moment, we become new human beings, and not only ordinary human beings entertaining new thoughts. New thoughts, new ideas, are finally not enough. It is a new mind itself that is needed in this life; and these meditations have the power to give us a taste of that. That is their secret power.

And, we may conclude, that is a first real step toward awakening from the troubled sleep of our lives.

But if, when you have come to the end . . . you honor only your guiding part and the divine that is within you, and you do not fear ceasing to live so much as you fear never having begun to live in accordance with Nature—then you will be a man who is worthy of the Cosmos that created you; and you will cease to live like a stranger in your own land. . . .

MEDITATIONS, 12.1

Historical Introduction

JOHN P. PIAZZA

The future emperor was born Marcus Annius Verus in A.D. 121, to the Roman aristocratic family Annia. He was named after his grandfather, who held the high office of consul (similar to that of prime minister in modern times) an almost unprecedented three times. Marcus' father, also named Verus, was also politically successful, holding the office of praetor and destined for the consulship, had he not died when Marcus was still an adolescent. As a result, Marcus recalled little of his father, with whom he spent meager time, but acknowledged that he did learn something from him: "From his reputation and my own memory of my father, modesty and strength."

During his early years, Marcus was under the care of his maternal great-grandfather Lucius Catilius Severus. The details of this man's influence on young Marcus are uncertain, but we know from the *Meditations* that Severus oversaw his early education, and took this matter very seriously, judging from the quality of education he helped provide for Marcus. Roman children of means began their formal education around age seven, when they would be tutored in both Latin and Greek, as well as placed in the care of a *tropheus,* a mentor of sorts, who accompanies the child and looks after his general moral well-being (see 1.5). At this time, he was also enrolled in the *Salii,* a religious troupe dedicated to the war-god Mars. The name comes from the Latin word *salire,* which means "to dance." This group would perform elaborate ritual dances in traditional Roman armor. Marcus soon distinguished himself by his piety and seriousness, becoming *vates,* or "prophet," which was the name for the leader of the dance. Legend has it that once when Marcus threw off his ceremonial crown at the end of a performance of the *Salii,* it landed directly on the head of a statue of Mars. This was later interpreted as an omen of his future rise to power.

At age twelve, Marcus began his secondary education, and by this time the emperor Hadrian had become aware of the solemn young Marcus, and gave him the nickname Verissimus, which is a pun on his name Verus and means "most truthful" or "most genuine." At this stage, Roman boys would learn geometry, music, and other more advanced subjects. Marcus was placed in the care of a teacher named Diognetus. His encounter with Diognetus can be seen as a milestone in that it was Marcus' first experience of a philosopher. At this point, we must distinguish philosophy as it is commonly known today, namely the study *of* philosophy, which happens on most college campuses, from the ancient notion, which is the *practice* of a particular way of life. To be a philosopher in Marcus' time was to dedicate oneself to a particular school and to adhere to its daily practices. Although these schools varied in doctrine, they all held this model to varying degrees. As Pierre Hadot points out in *The Inner Citadel*, there are many who studied and even wrote about philosophy but who would never have been called philosophers. This is because the ancient measure of a philosopher was not his discourses, but his way of living.

In Diognetus, Marcus found an early *exemplum*, a person in whom he could observe and begin to emulate the habits of the philosophically-minded. This included thinking critically about commonly accepted Roman activities; practicing a healthy skepticism with regard to those who claim to perform miracles and exorcisms; exposing oneself to philosophical ideas; and finally "to aspire to the simple cloak and sleeping-cot and other accessories of the Greek training." This last lesson, which he claims to have learned from Diognetus, is further evidence that for Marcus philosophy was anything but an armchair pursuit. Several years remained before the world of Roman politics would begin to exercise its pull on the nascent leader. But even then, Marcus would continue to pursue his studies and practices.

By the year A.D. 138, Emperor Hadrian's unreliable health caused him to consider carefully his next heir. He began to take steps, specifically an arranged marriage and a politically motivated adoption, to ensure that Marcus would eventually reach the throne, though not until after the long reign of his adoptive father, Antoninus Pius. As a result of these initial political machinations, Marcus was moved into the imperial palace—much to the frustration of his self-imposed philosophic austerity. But this abrupt change contained a blessing for Marcus, for he came into contact with the philosopher Apollonius of Chalcedon, one of the leading expounders of Stoic philosophy. As we can see from Marcus' comments in Book One of the *Meditations*, Apollonius had a profound and lasting influence on Marcus' life as another philosophical *exemplum*. With the help of Apollonius, Marcus would continue his pursuit of the philosophic way of life, even in the tempting atmosphere of the imperial palace.

War and Plague: A.D. 161—180

Soon after his succession, Marcus was faced with the prospect of defending the Empire's large territory from invading tribes to the north and east. Militarily, he was more or less successful in holding back the tide of invaders. Within a few years, however, Roman forces were succumbing to another enemy, in the form of a plague, which soldiers returning to their homes in the Roman provinces were spreading throughout the Empire. This plague, one of the worst in memory, would severely compromise Rome's ability to defend itself against future military attacks, which would continue for Marcus' entire reign.

Between A.D. 167 and his death in 180, observers say, Marcus spent most of his time directly overseeing the military campaigns on the Empire's northern borders. It is during this period that Marcus felt compelled to write his philosophical reminders to himself, to recall his early training in a philosophical way of life, and to put that training into practice in the midst of profoundly trying circumstances. It is important for readers of the *Meditations* to remember that Marcus was not writing in the comfort of his royal palace, but in spare moments while conducting a series of campaigns which stretched over a decade. From this perspective, the value of Marcus' short book becomes clear, as well as the reasons behind its somewhat austere tone of resignation to forces beyond one's control. Marcus was probably aware that he would spend the rest of his life waging war far from his home and family. In A.D. 180 it was believed that Marcus himself—Rome's highest citizen—succumbed to plague, lending grim credence to Marcus' repeated claims in the *Meditations* that nobody, regardless of personal rank, is immune to the forces of nature.

Marcus' Thought

Marcus' *Meditations* is among the best known and most widely read works of antiquity. The book continues to find new readers today, nearly two thousand years after it was written. What is this remarkably enduring work about? It is first and foremost an inner exploration, a record of Marcus' dialogue with himself regarding the problems and questions of life, questions that any philosopher faces. It confronts head-on the problems associated with living and acting in an imperfect world filled with circumstances beyond one's control without abandoning one's principles. It testifies against the common notion that philosophy is a solitary or even indulgent activity, given the difficulties in the world and our pressing obligations toward others. By contrast, the writings of the great philosophers, and those of Marcus in particular, show how notions of inner self-knowledge and outer right-action are inseparable. A famous quote from Plato's *Republic* can serve to remind us of this important connection:

> Unless either philosophers become kings, or those who are now called kings seriously and adequately take up the pursuit of philosophy, and unless there is a union of these two things, namely political power and philosophy, then there can be no relief from troubles, my dear Glaucon, for our cities, nor, I fear, for the whole human race.

Marcus Aurelius was one of the great heirs to this Platonic tradition, in that he lived most of his adult life surrounded by politics, power, and war—but he was continually anchored and strengthened by his philosophical training.

Not once in the *Meditations* does Marcus refer to himself as an emperor, general, philosopher, or any of those roles for which he was famous and respected. It soon becomes clear that he is not writing from the perspective of any particular identity, doctrine, or philosophical school. So what is he doing—what is the practice of his "meditations"? Is it a matter of philosophy, in a modern sense, or of religion, mysticism, psychology, spirituality, or politics? It is not any of these in particular, yet his exhortations to himself touch on all of these areas in very powerful ways. In his refusal to call himself anything but a Roman and a human being, Marcus seems to be investigating human life and his own life by stripping the human being down to two absolutely essential elements. These are *mind* and *participation* in a society with other human beings.

At root, Marcus sees mind as the source of human freedom, for it is only with the help of the mind that we can begin to step back from our often thoughtless reactions to our surroundings and view them from a different perspective, and only then perhaps begin to change our lives. He repeatedly writes that every human being has within himself an ability to be free from the suffering that results from the tyranny of our emotional responses. This is, however, a power that most of us do not realize we possess, because we have experienced it haphazardly if at all. In addition, nobody has taught us that this different way of thinking and experiencing ourselves in the world can and must be cultivated. In the course of his own inner searching, Marcus is giving us an opportunity to witness the workings of our own minds, to really know and use this capacity for stepping back and becoming truly aware of who we are, what we are doing, and the reasons for our actions. This ability, argues Marcus, is the only way to freedom. Only in using it, he asserts, may we join together with others and begin to form a real society, something he calls *a community of the mind.*

The Philosophy: Stoicism

We must begin our discussion of Marcus Aurelius' philosophy by noting that he never calls himself a Stoic, although history has associated him with that way of thought (which we will shortly examine). The *Meditations* is not a philosophical treatise. Nor is the author asserting an ideology or a system of government. What we have instead are the words of a man writing to no one but himself, as he saw himself: not as an emperor or philosopher but as an individual human being. Marcus seems to be trying, above all, to free his mind from the bonds of all categories, be they political, religious, or even philosophical. In spite of his obviously Stoic influences, Marcus refers not to Epictetus the Stoic but to Epictetus the man, the teacher. And he does not hesitate to cite others, regardless of their philosophical school, if they have something important to contribute. Having said this, let us now look at what is called Stoicism.

The philosophical school known as Stoicism was founded in Athens in the fourth century B.C. by the philosopher Zeno of Citium. The names "stoicism" and "stoic" come from the *stoa poikile* (painted porch) where Zeno would meet with his students. In the *agora* (main square) at Athens, there sat a number of porches or porticos, which provided shade and shelter for participants in various public exchanges, from markets to religious ceremonies. Historical sources say that Zeno's *stoa* was adorned by the best painters of the day with scenes depicting the most famous historical and mythological episodes of the Greeks.

Stoicism can be understood as beginning with a broad conception of the nature of the human being and his place in the world. The entire cosmos (which, in Greek, means "beauty" and "order" in addition to "universe") is organized by an ordering force, or *logos.* The human being also contains such an organizing or guiding element, which is called "mind" or "reason." Human life, therefore, has a specific context in which it exists—and can potentially thrive. This, however, depends upon the extent to which an individual lives "in accordance with nature." As a first task, this means recognizing what is within our control and acting within that relatively limited sphere, rather than wasting our energy and frustrations on circumstances we cannot change. The second task requires approaching the rest of life—that which is out of our control—with an attitude of indifference or even acceptance. When humans live in this way, the Stoics hold, they are most happy, for they are not tormented with anxiety over circumstances they cannot change. Cultivating such an attitude in the daily practice of living requires constant attention and reminders.

Roman Stoicism: Marcus' Influences

Early Stoicism defined itself in opposition to other philosophical schools, including those of Plato and Aristotle. But the later Stoicism of the Roman Republic and Empire adopted a much more conciliatory tone, as its practitioners strove to make their philosophy appealing to a wide general audience. As a result, we see in Roman Stoicism an effort to emphasize commonalities of doctrine among traditionally rival philosophical schools. In addition, because these later Stoic writings were aimed at a broad Roman readership and not just adherents to the school and because the Roman temperament was oriented more toward action than contemplation for its own sake, we see in these popular writings a shift away from the particularities of doctrine and toward the description of, and exhortation to, a philosophic way of life. Seneca the Younger (d. A.D. 65) is a primary example of this philosophical attitude. A powerful and wealthy Roman politician, Seneca published a series of letters to a young man, Lucilius, to whom Seneca was a mentor. In these letters, Seneca addresses the many challenges of living a philosophical life amid the busyness and temptations of Roman society. His letters focus almost entirely on the practical application of Stoic principles; as a result, this work has remained immensely popular almost since it was written, no doubt influencing not only Marcus but also later emulators, in particular the essayists Montaigne, Pascal, and Emerson.

Probably the most influential writer for Marcus was Epictetus. Epictetus was born a slave in the first century A.D. Later freed by his master, Epictetus went on to study philosophy, becoming an adherent, then an expositor and innovator, of the Stoic school. His innovation appeared not so much in the area of doctrine, but in a singular emphasis on the critical need to apply the principles of Stoicism to one's everyday life. His surviving works consist of a collection of Greek discourses, or lectures, which were written down by his pupil Arrian, in which he exhorts his students, often through Socratic cross-examination, to avoid the academic temptation of learning merely for its own sake. The dominant themes of his work are self-awareness, controlling one's emotional reactions to circumstances, and the cultivation of an ability to distinguish between that which is and is not within one's power. The *Meditations* contains many references, direct and indirect, to Epictetus' work, and it is clearly the chief written literary influence on Marcus. That the Roman emperor chose to compose his *Meditations* in Greek, and in a style which emulates that of Epictetus' discourses, is further evidence of the profound influence exercised by Epictetus' writings.

The Book

This edition is intended as an introduction to Marcus Aurelius, and so we have selected those passages from the *Meditations* that we believe convey the universal significance of his thought for people in all walks of life. In choosing which passages to include, we have been guided by the aim of making Marcus' writings as accessible as possible to a general audience.

In his discussion of the *Meditations*, Pierre Hadot notes that "philosophy, like poetry, is untranslatable." This calls attention to one key characteristic of the *Meditations*: it was written in Greek. We must remember that Marcus, like all educated Romans of his time, was raised bilingually in both Latin and Greek. While Latin was both his mother tongue and the official language of the Empire, Latin was widely considered limited when it came to the technical vocabulary of philosophy, law, and the sciences—and thus the need to know Greek. Greek, by contrast, was the language of philosophy, and to translate its specific terminology into Latin was to water it down to some degree. It is therefore no mystery that Marcus wrote his meditations in Greek.

The more time we have spent with the *Meditations*, the more convinced we have become of the depth of Marcus' philosophical expression. This acquaintance with the *Medita-*

tions has shown us that Marcus was anything but a leader who merely dabbled in philosophy. Rather, we have been repeatedly humbled by the depth of his capacity for philosophical thought and reflection within a specific and intentional framework. For all the independence of the author's thought, the *Meditations* in its language, style, and method reflects a formal model, rooted in a specific tradition. Hadot describes this well when he notes in *The Inner Citadel*: "The Meditations are not spontaneous effusions, but exercises carried out in accordance with a program which Marcus had received from the Stoic tradition, and in particular from Epictetus. Marcus was working with pre-existing materials, and painting on a canvas given him by someone else."

This insight, combined with the notion that Marcus was almost certainly writing for himself alone (the earliest title attributed to the work is "To Himself"), helps to explain many of the difficulties that readers, translators, and scholars have encountered in the text. Indeed, the *Meditations* contains many obscurities, and the style is pointed, compact, and often lacking in background information. To the informed reader, however, it is clear that the *Meditations* was not written in a vacuum, but rather forms part of his response to the pressures and obligations of his role as emperor, and cannot be understood separate from these circumstances.

We are unashamed to acknowledge that we encountered many passages which we were unable to understand fully, much less convey in English to a general audience, without a great deal of research and commentary. Therefore, rather than filling this book with notes or, worse, simplifying Marcus' words in the interests of an empty comprehensibility, we have chosen simply to omit such passages. We have, however, retained the traditional order and numbering of the chapters and indicated with an asterisk (*) chapters from which we have made omissions, in the hope that the reader, if so inclined, will be able to consult complete translations and secondary sources in order to explore these ideas further.

The
Text

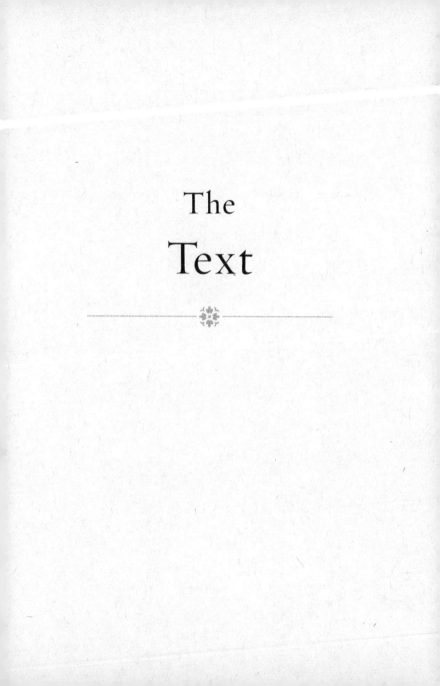

Book One

❀

1.1
From my grandfather Verus, I learned about nobility of character and a steady temper.

1.2
From his reputation and my own memory of my father, modesty and strength.

1.3
From my mother, devotion to the gods, generosity, and that one should turn away not only from hurtful actions, but even from the very thought of them; also, simplicity in one's way of living, far removed from the self-indulgent ways of the wealthy.

1.4*
From my great-grandfather, the need to have good teachers at home, and to know that one should spare no expense on such things.

1.5

From my tutor, not to side with either team at the chariot races, nor to be a partisan of either side at the gladiator fights; from him too I learned about enduring difficulties, requiring little, doing my own labor, not meddling in other people's affairs, and to resist the temptation of listening to slander.

1.6 *

From Diognetus, not to be excited by trifling things, not to take seriously what is said by fortune tellers about incantations and the exorcising of spirits and other such things; not to breed fighting quail, nor to get excited over such things; to endure loose-talkers; to make philosophy my home, to write philosophical dialogues as a young man, and to desire only a simple cot and animal skin for my bed, and only what is necessary for the Greek discipline of philosophy.

1.7

From Rusticus, the realization that my character is in need of rehabilitation and care; not to be distracted by purely rhetorical exercises, write treatises full of moral generalizations, spew forth trite sentences of exhortation, or glorify with literary ornamentation either the hermit or the do-gooder. To stay away from rhetorical and poetic display, or an affected city snobbery. Not to parade around my household in ceremonial dress, nor anything of this sort. Rather, to write letters in a plain and sincere style, like the one he wrote to my mother from Sinuessa. Also, to be eager for reconciliation and mediation with anyone who, having lost their temper and caused trouble, wishes to return. To read with precision and not be satisfied with the mere gist of things, nor to agree too quickly with clever debaters. Finally, to have encountered the discourses of Epictetus, which he provided for me from his own library.

1.8

From the philosopher Apollonius, true freedom, and an absolute resolve not to place my hopes in mere chance; and to keep my eyes fixed on nothing else—without even a moment's distraction—except Reason; to remain always the same, during terrible pains, the loss of my child,[1] or during long bouts of illness; and to see clearly in Apollonius living proof that a person can be both fully engaged and at peace, never impatient while teaching, and to see in him a person who clearly considered his great practical experience and his talent in expounding philosophical theories as least among those things that make a man good. From him I also learned how to accept so-called favors from acquaintances without being completely

---

1. Only one of Marcus' five children lived long enough to succeed him.

indebted to them because of these favors, or letting them go unnoticed and disrespected.

1.9

From Sextus, graciousness, and an example of what it means to lead a household like a true father. Also, an understanding of what it means to live one's life according to Nature; to carry oneself with dignity, but not as if wearing a mask; unintrusive concern for friends, and a tolerance for the foolish, and for those whose ideas have not been thought out. Such a harmonious nature that, although his company was sweeter than flattery, he nevertheless had the effect of arousing the utmost respect in others. Skill and precision in the arrangement of guiding principles, which are essential for life. Never to reveal that he was harboring anger or any other emotional reaction, but to be unaffected—yet at the same time displaying genuine affection. To give praise without flattery, and how to be extremely learned without being a show-off.

1.10

From Alexander, the scholar of Greek literature and oratory, never to indulge in gratuitous criticism of others; never to ridicule those who have let slip some unrefined, provincial or ugly phrase, but rather to respond tactfully and offer the correct expression within a reply or a supporting argument, or even a joint investigation of the matter itself—though not the mistake—or some other suitable way of reminding them without pointing it out directly.

1.11

From Fronto, the understanding that envy, deceit and hypocrisy are common traits of a leader. Also, that we Patricians are, on the whole, incapable of expressing friendly affection.

1.12

From Alexander the Platonist, to say or write in a letter rarely and only when necessary that I have no time to spare; nor to use urgent business as an excuse to avoid obligations which are required by those around us.

1.13

From the philosopher Catulus, never to be dismissive of a friend's accusation, even if it seems unreasonable, but to make every effort to restore the relationship to its normal condition. Also to commend with sincerity and enthusiasm one's teachers, as in the writings about Domitius and Athenodotus. Finally, to have true affection for one's children.

1.14 *

From my brother-in-law Severus, love of family, truth and justice; the ability to entertain the idea of a government in which all are equal under the same laws, and which is administered according to equal rights and freedom of speech; the idea of a monarchy which values most of all the freedom of its subjects. Also, a constant and unwavering esteem for philosophy, and an eagerness to help others, to be optimistic, and to trust in the love of friends.

1.15*

From Maximus, how to rule over oneself and never to be "carried away" by anything. Also, a positive outlook in difficult circumstances, especially illness. How to conduct oneself in a gentle and dignified way; the accomplishment of necessary duties without complaint. Everyone trusted that he said what he thought and that he never did anything without good reasons. Never taken off-guard or panicked; never hurried, hesitant, undecided, or exhibiting a false kindness—nor on the other hand was he angry, irritable, or suspicious. Helpful and generous, forgiving and honest. To present oneself as one who cannot be corrupted in the first place, rather than as a reformed man propped up by external assistance. Finally, that nobody would think that he was looking down upon them, but nor would they dare to think themselves superior to him.

1.16*

From my adoptive father, Antoninus Pius, mildness of temper, unshakable resolution in matters which he had determined after due deliberation; to have no empty vanity with respect to so-called honors; a love of work and perseverance; and a willingness to hear any suggestions for the good of the community. Also, an undeviating determination to give each person their fair share; and to know from experience when to exert oneself and when to let go. In addition, how to make use of the many things Fortune provides which contribute to the comfort of life, modestly and without apology, so as simply to enjoy them when they are present and not to miss them when they are gone.

Importantly, to acknowledge without envy those who have special ability, be it in matters of public speaking, law, custom, or anything else, even sharing in their enthusiasm so that each might be esteemed for their particular gifts. Also, to do everything according to the traditions of our ancestors but never merely for the sake of public display.

One might apply to him what was said of Socrates, that he was able to abstain from those things which most people are too weak to abstain from, and enjoy what most people cannot enjoy without excess. But to be strong and persistent in each case is characteristic of someone who has a perfected and unconquerable soul.

1.17 *

I am grateful to the gods for good grandfathers, good parents, a good sister, good teachers, good companions, good family and friends, and nearly everything good. Further, I am grateful that I did not offend any of them, although I was of such a disposition which might have caused me to do something of the sort, if given the opportunity; but thanks to the gods' favor, there was no such combination of circumstances so as to put me to such a test. Also, that I was subordinate to a ruler and father who could rid me of all pride and help me realize that a man can live in a royal palace without wanting guards, embroidered clothing, torches, statues, or other such things, but rather, to realize that it is within such a man's power to bring himself as close as possible to the condition of an ordinary citizen, yet without becoming more base or indifferent toward matters of state, which must be handled in a kingly manner. I am also thankful to the gods that I had clear and frequent conceptions about what it means to live in accordance with Nature, so that there was nothing to prevent me from beginning straightaway to live according to Nature, though I still fall short of this goal through my own fault and through my ignorance of the reminders, or rather direct instructions, of the gods. I am also thankful that, once I had an appetite for philosophy, I did not fall into the hands of some so-called wise man, and that I did not waste my time publishing or attempting to solve logical puzzles, or busy myself with observing the sky.

Book Two

2.1

Begin each day by saying to yourself: Today I am going to encounter people who are ungrateful, arrogant, deceitful, envious, and hostile. People have these characteristics because they do not understand what is good and what is bad. But insofar as I have comprehended the true nature of what is good, namely that it is fine and noble, and the true nature of what is bad, that it is shameful, and the true nature of the person who has gone astray: that he is just like me, not only in the physical sense but also with respect to Intelligence and having a portion of the divine—insofar as I have comprehended all this, I can neither be harmed by any of them, for no one else can involve me in what is shameful and debasing, nor can I be angry with my fellow man or hate him, for we have been made for cooperation, just like the feet, the hands, the eyelids, and the upper and lower teeth. To hinder one another, then, is contrary to Nature, and this is exactly what happens when we are angry and turn away from each other.

2.4

Remember how long you have been putting these things off, and how often you have received an opportunity from the gods and have not made use of it. By now you ought to realize what cosmos you are a part of, and what divine administrator you owe your existence to, and that an end to your time here has been marked out, and if you do not use this time for clearing the clouds from your mind, it will be gone, and so will you.

2.5

Each and every hour make up your mind steadfastly as a Roman and as a man to accomplish the matter presently at hand with genuine solemnity, loving care, independence, and justice, and to provide yourself with relief from all other worries; and you will achieve this if you perform every action in your life as if it were your last, putting aside all aimlessness and emotional resistance to the choices of reason, and all pretense, selfishness, and discontent with what has been allotted to you. See how few are the things which a person must gain control of in order to live a peaceful and godlike existence, for the gods will ask nothing more from the person who does so.

2.6

Go ahead, soul, be destructive, but you may not have another opportunity to honor yourself, for each person has only one life—and yours is almost finished; yet you still do not respect yourself, but locate your own happiness in the minds of others.

2.8

Not easily will you find a person who is unhappy due to ignorance of what goes on in another person's soul; but those who do not follow the movements of their own soul will surely be unhappy.

2.9

You must always keep this in mind: What is the nature of the Whole? what is my nature? and how is my nature related to that greater Nature? Also, that nobody can hinder you from constantly doing and saying what is in keeping with Nature, of which you are a part.

2.12*

How quickly all things disappear, both the things themselves in the universe and, in time, even their memory. As for the things we perceive through the senses, which entice us with physical pleasure or terrify us with pain, or make us famous through rumor, how worthless, contemptible, filthy, short-lived, or indeed already dead they are! Intelligence alone can understand this, as well as what kind of people they truly are whose opinions and voices make reputations. Also, if one sees death for what it is, and with the power of Intelligence strips away all its imaginary characteristics, one will then understand death to be nothing more than a natural process, and it is childish to be afraid of a natural process. Moreover, this is not only a natural process, but is for the well-being of Nature herself.

2.13

Nothing is more pathetic than the person who goes around and around, inquiring into things below the earth, as the saying goes, and strives to understand the workings of his neighbor's mind, without perceiving that he need only look to the divine spirit within himself, and care for it sincerely. And caring means keeping it pure of suffering, aimlessness, and discontent with anything divine or human that should happen, for whatever comes from the gods should be revered on account of their inherent excellence, and things done by humans should be met with kindness because of the kinship we all share. But sometimes human deeds deserve our compassion. This is because people are ignorant of what is good and what is bad, which is no less a disability than the inability to distinguish white from black.

2.14

Even if you should live three thousand years, or thirty thousand for that matter, know just the same that no one loses any other life than the one he now lives, nor does one live any other life than that which he will lose. The longest and shortest lives thus amount to the same, for the present moment is equal for everyone, and what we lose turns out never to have belonged to us in the first place; and so what has been lost is only a mere moment. Nobody can lose either the past or the future, for how can anyone lose what they never possessed? Therefore, these two things must be remembered: first, that all things are eternally of the same form, and they recur in cycles. Therefore, it makes no difference whether a person sees these same things repeated in a hundred years, or two hundred, or in an infinite amount of time. Second, that the longest to live and the soonest to die lose exactly the same thing, for it is only the present moment which one can be deprived of, if it is true that we possess this alone, and that you cannot lose what you do not have.

2.17 *

The duration of a person's life is only a moment; our substance is flowing away this very moment; the senses are dim; the composition of the body is decaying, the soul is chaos, our fate is unknowable, and reputation uncertain. In a word, all bodily things are like a flowing river, and everything of the soul is dream and smoke, and life is all warfare and a stranger's wanderings, and the reward is oblivion. What then could possibly guide us? Only one thing: philosophy, and this consists in keeping the divine spirit within each of us free from disrespect and harm, above pains and pleasures, doing nothing aimlessly or falsely and with pretense, without need of another's doing or not doing something, and, furthermore, accepting all that may happen and is allotted to us as coming from that source, whatever it is, from which we ourselves came. Also, philosophy consists in awaiting death with a contented mind, as nothing other than a liberation of those elements of which a living being is composed.

Book Three

❦

3.2

We should closely observe the following: even the incidental by-products of natural processes have some pleasure and allure. For example, when bread is being baked, certain parts of it split open, and these parts which are split open in such a way, and are in a sense incidental to the breadmaker's art, have a certain appropriateness and, strangely, they even stimulate an appetite for food. Figs, too, when they are at their ripest, gape open. And in the case of very ripe olives, their very nearness to rotting, strangely, is what gives them a certain beauty. The same is true for full stalks of wheat bending downward, the lion's furled brow, the foam dripping from the boar's mouth, and many other things which, while far from beautiful when seen in isolation, nevertheless adorn and beautify these processes and entice our minds because they follow from the workings of Nature.

Therefore, if a person has a deep feeling for and a deep understanding of the workings of the Whole, there is hardly anything that will not seem to be composed in a way that is pleasurable to contemplate, even though it may exist only as an incidental by-product. And so such a person will even look upon the actual gaping jaws of beasts with no less pleasure than when he admires the beasts which painters and sculptors display through the art of representation. He will discern in the elderly a certain mature prime and seasonableness and, in children, will be able to see with decent eyes their beautiful allure. Many such things are not attractive to everyone, but only to that person who has become genuinely intimate with Nature and its workings.

3.3 *

Hippocrates, after healing so many sick people, became sick himself and died. The Chaldeans prophesized countless deaths, and yet their own dark prophecies caught up even with them. What does all this mean? It means that you have boarded your ship, you have set sail, and that you have made it to your destination: now step ashore. If, on the one hand, you go on to another life, that life will not be lacking in gods. If, on the other hand, it is mere unconsciousness, then you will no longer be at the mercy of pains and pleasures as a servant to this earthly vessel.

3.4

Do not waste what remains of your life with anxiety about others, unless you can elevate those thoughts and bring them in relation to some common good. For otherwise you will surely neglect some other important task, when you worry in this way about what some clever person is doing and why, what he is saying, what he has in mind, what he is contriving, and all such thoughts and worries which distract you from keeping watch over *your* guiding part.

Therefore we should not only avoid aimlessness and idleness in the series of our thoughts, but, most of all, whatever is overly inquisitive and of bad character. And you should accustom yourself to think only of those things which, if someone were suddenly to ask "What are you thinking?" you could openly answer this or that, so as to reveal straightaway that everything within yourself is straightforward and well disposed, appropriate to a communal being, and without care for base pleasures or even a single one of the delights we take in our experiences or for any rivalry, slander, suspicion, or anything else which you would blush to answer that you had in your mind.

Such a person, no longer hesitant to assume his rightful place among the noblest, becomes a kind of priest or assistant to the gods, insofar as he tends to that interior divinity which alone can make a person uncorrupted by pleasures, unaffected by pain, unharmed by outrageous behavior, and insensitive to any sort of malice. He is a contender in the greatest competition of all: the struggle not to be overthrown by our emotions. He has been dipped deep in the dye of justice, welcoming with his entire soul all that will come to pass as his assigned portion. Rarely if ever, unless required by some urgent communal necessity, does he busy himself with what someone else is saying, doing, or thinking, for he is focused on doing what is required of him, and he thinks only of those duties and circumstances which, of everything in the universe, have been spun by Fate for him alone. He strives to make them noble and beautiful, for he is convinced that they are good. This is because each person's guiding part not only directs that person, but is itself directed by something higher.

And such a person does not forget that all things which come from Reason share the same nature, and that it is in accordance with our nature to care for all people; also that the mere opinion of the many should not be adopted, but rather the opinion of those alone who live in open agreement with Nature. But in regard to those who do not live in this way, of what sort they are at home and abroad, by night and by day, and what company they keep, he remains constantly mindful. As a result, he thinks nothing of praise from such people, who in fact are not even content with themselves.

3.5

Neither unwillingly, selfishly, nor in an unexamined or distracted way should you go about your business. Do not embellish your thoughts with a lot of refinement. Do not run your mouth off or be a busybody. Moreover, let the divine part within you be ruler and guardian of a living being that is brave, mature, caring for his community, a true Roman, and a ruler who has taken up his position in the manner of a soldier who awaits the call to give up his life, requiring no oath or witness of anyone. Be cheerful, without dependence on the external support or ease which companions can provide. One must stand upright and not be propped up.

3.6

If you should find anything better in human life than justice, truth, self-control, courage, and, in a word, your mind's contentment with itself in those things which it empowers you to practice in accordance with Reason, and to be contented with what has been allotted to you without any choice—if, I say, you see anything better than this, then with all your heart turn to it and take pleasure in that which you have discovered to be best of all. But if there seems to be nothing better than that very spirit which has been placed in you, and which, as Socrates said, gives us the ability to examine impressions,[2] and the ability to tear itself away from the persuasions of the senses, and to submit itself to the gods, and to care for others—if you should find all other things smaller and of lesser value than this, do not give pride of place to anything else, toward which, if you should even once be turned and then be inclined toward them, you will no longer be able to honor without distraction what is good and what most properly belongs to you. For it

---

2. Marcus is applying Epictetus' interpretation to a famous saying of Socrates. "For just as Socrates used to say that the unexamined life is not worth living, in this way we should never simply accept an impression that we have not scrutinized, but say to it: 'Just a minute; let me see what you are and where you come from.' " Epictetus, *Discourses*, 3.12.15.

is not sanctioned by the gods that anything else, such as the praise of the many, power, wealth, or indulgence in pleasures should be placed above what is in accordance with Reason and the communal good. All such things, even if they may seem for a little while to fit in with what is higher, can suddenly overpower us and sweep us away at any time.

Simply and freely choose what is better and hold your ground. "But whatever is to my advantage must be the best," you might say. If it is to your advantage as a rational being, then hold on to it; but if it is to your advantage as a mere animate creature, admit this with humility. Only make sure you have made a choice that is not dishonorable.

3.7

Never consider anything to be beneficial to you, which could ever compel you to violate your faith in yourself, to abandon your modesty, to hate anybody, to be overly suspicious, cursing, disingenuous, or to lust after anything which must be hidden behind walls or veils. For the person who has chosen his own intelligence and inner spirit, and the sacred reveling in this kind of excellence, does not play a tragic role, does not groan with lament, and has no need of either complete solitude or excessive company. Most important, such a person will live life neither chasing it nor fleeing from it. Also, such a person does not care at all whether his soul is kept contained in the body for a long or short span of time, for even if he must depart at once, he will do this exactly as he would accomplish any deed which can be done in a self-respecting and orderly manner, throughout one's life watching out for this alone: that the mind not adopt a manner of life unfit for a thinking and communal being.

3.9

Revere your capacity for making decisions. Everything depends on this alone, so that your guiding part does not make a decision that is contrary either to Nature or to your makeup as a being endowed with reason. This demands freedom from rash judgments, fellowship with others, and obedience toward the gods.

3.10

Once you have cast off everything else, hold fast to these few principles alone.[3] Also remember that each person lives in this very moment, and that the rest either has already happened or else is entirely uncertain. Small indeed is the life which each person lives, and tiny is the corner of the earth where he lives. Small too is even the longest after-glory, which is handed off, as in a relay race, to others who will soon be dead, not having known even themselves, let alone someone who died long ago.

---

3. I.e., those which have been mentioned above.

3.11*

Nothing is so productive of greatness of mind as the ability to examine systematically and truthfully each thing we encounter in life, and to see these things in such a way as to comprehend the nature of the Cosmos, and what sort of benefit such things possess for both the Whole and for humans, all of whom are citizens of the most supreme City, that is, the entire world, compared to which all actual cities are like mere households. This thing or circumstance that now gives me an impression: What is it? What is it made of? How long will it last? And, most important, what quality does it require of me, such as gentleness, courage, honesty, faith, simplicity, independence, and the like?

Therefore it is necessary in each case to say the following: this circumstance has come from god and is in keeping with fate or with coincidence; while this other circumstance is caused by a relative and neighbor, though such a person is ignorant of what his nature requires of him. But I am not ignorant, and therefore I will treat them well and justly, according to the natural law which governs any community. At the same time, in morally neutral matters I will work with them in pursuit of what is right.

3.13

Just as doctors always keep their implements and scalpels ready at hand in case of an emergency treatment, so should you have your guiding principles ready in order to understand things human and divine, and for the doing of everything, even the smallest deed, being aware at all times of the bond that unites these two realms. For you can never do anything well which concerns humans unless you consult the divine; nor can you do anything well concerning the divine without first consulting the human realm.

Book Four

❧

4.1

That power which rules us from inside, when it is in its natural state, stands in such a way in relation to whatever may happen that it easily adapts itself at all times both to its own capabilities and what it has been given by fate. For it is not attracted toward one kind of material thing or event but adapts itself to all internal and external limitations, whether those limitations are due to ability or fate. Nevertheless, it converts into usable fuel anything that opposes it, just as fire does when it consumes what is thrown upon it, by which a small fire would have been extinguished. But a blazing fire quickly assimilates to itself whatever is cast upon it, engulfing it as fuel and rising even higher because of it.

4.3*

People seek retreats for themselves in the country, by the sea, and near the mountains; and you too are especially prone to desire such things. But this is a sign of ignorance, since you have the power to retire within yourself whenever you wish.

For nowhere can a person retire more full of peace and free from care than into one's own soul; above all, if one has that place within oneself into which one can turn one's attention, one is immediately at ease. And by ease I mean nothing other than the right ordering of the whole person. Continually give yourself this kind of retreat and regenerate yourself, but keep your rules of living brief and basic so that, when consulted, they will immediately wash away all distress and send you back to your work without resentment.

What is it that disturbs you? Human evil? Recall this truth to your mind: rational beings have come into existence for the sake of each other; and tolerance and patience are aspects of what it means to be just; and people do not do wrong intentionally. Also, consider how many people, having lived in enmity, suspicion, hatred, and combat—how many have been laid out as corpses and reduced to ashes. Recall this, and cease your discontent.

But will you let mere fame distract you? Turn your gaze to the quick forgetfulness of all things, the abyss of the ages on either side of this present moment, and the empty echo of praise, the transitory quality and lack of judgment on the part of those who praise, and the tiny area in which all this is confined. For the entire Earth is only a mere point in the universe, and what a small corner of the Earth is our dwelling place; and in that place, see how few and of what sort are the people who celebrate you!

For the time that remains, remember the humble refuge

which is yourself. And, above all, do not be anxious or overextend yourself, but be truly independent and see circumstances from the perspective of a man, of a human being, of a citizen, a creature who will surely die. But among the thoughts that are closest at hand, which you will look to, let these two be there: first, that various difficulties need not penetrate to your soul but can remain external, unaffecting—such disturbances come from nothing other than your internal judgments; second, remember that all the things which you now see are changing and will not continue to exist as they are. Continually bear in mind how many changes you have already witnessed. The Cosmos is constant change, and our lives are but a series of choices.

4.4*

If the capacity of intellect is common to us all, then Reason, in virtue of which we are all thinking beings, is also common to us all. And if this is the case, then Law, too, is common; and if this is so, then we are citizens. If this is so, then we all have a share in some sort of community. If this is true, then the Cosmos is a kind of city-state, as it were, for what other single community can one say the whole of mankind belongs to? And this common city-state is the very source of the intellect itself, as well as the powers of reasoning and lawgiving, or where else do you think these faculties could possibly come from?

The Essential Marcus Aurelius

4.11

Do not hold the same views as the person who does you harm, or even wishes to harm you. Rather, see these judgments for what they truly are.

4.17

Do not live as if you still have ten thousand years left. Your fate hangs over you. While you are still living, while you still exist on this Earth, strive to become a genuinely good man.

4.18

What an abundance of leisure the person gains who is not looking over at what his neighbor is saying, doing, or thinking, but only at what he himself is doing, in order that he does what is just and respectful of the gods. As Agathon[4] said, do not peer into the darkness of another's character, but run straight toward the finish line without straying from your path.

4.19

The person who pines after some sort of lasting fame does not realize that each person who remembers him will themselves soon be dead; and then the person who continues the memory from them, until all memory of the person is extinguished as

---

4. Agathon (born circa 450 B.C.) is the celebrated tragic playwright, as well as political figure, who is portrayed in the comedies of Aristophanes and the dialogues of Plato, in particular the *Symposium*.

though in a relay race, in which the torch goes out right after it flares up. But even suppose that those who remember you might be immortal, and so the memory will be immortal. What good is that to you? I shouldn't even have to mention that all this is worth nothing to a dead man. But what good is it even to the living, except in some inconsequential way? For you forsake the opportunity afforded by your natural human gifts, in order to grasp onto the future gossip of others.

4.20

Everything which results in something beautiful is itself beautiful and is complete in itself, with praise holding no essential role. Therefore, whatever is praised becomes neither better nor worse because it is or is not praised. I assert this also of things which are commonly called beautiful, such as material things and the various arts and crafts. Does that which is beautiful really need anything in addition? No—no more than Law does; no more than Truth; no more than kindness, than modesty. Which of these is beautiful or ugly on account of being either praised or slandered? Does an emerald become ugly if it is not admired? What about gold, ivory, royal purple dye, the lyre, the sword, or a flower?

4.23

Everything that is in harmony with you has been so tuned in me, O Cosmos! Nothing in me is too early or late, as long as it is on time for you. All is nourishment for me, which your seasons bring, O Nature; all things come from you, all things subsist in you, and all things will return to you. One might say "Dear city of Cecrops." But will you not say "Dear city of Zeus"?[5]

4.24

It has been said, "If you want to be content, occupy yourself with few things." But it is perhaps better to say "Do what is necessary, and what Reason requires of a creature who is made for society—do whatever it demands." For this brings the contentment which comes from doing things well, and doing only a few things. Since most of what we say and do is entirely unnecessary, if a person could get rid of these, he would have more leisure and be in less of a state of confusion. Therefore we all must remember to ask ourselves: "Is this one of the truly necessary things?" But we must leave aside not only unnecessary activities but even unnecessary thoughts, so that unnecessary activities do not follow from them.

4.27[*]

Either the Cosmos has been arranged in an entirely well-ordered way, or has come together by chance, but nevertheless

---

5. The contrast here is between a particular city's divinity, Cecrops, the mythical founder of Athens, and Zeus, who is the god of all humankind. This is in keeping with the Stoic notion of a world-state, which unites rather than divides people.

remains an ordered whole, a Cosmos. Or do you think some kind of cosmic order can exist in you, while the Cosmos itself is chaos?

4.29*

He is like an open sore[6] on the Cosmos, who stands apart and separates himself from his natural communal Reason because he is displeased with his circumstances. For that same communal Reason brings those about as well, and it also produced you. He is an amputation from the community who severs his own soul from that of other reasoning beings, since it is all a unity.

4.30

One person philosophizes though he lacks a tunic, another without a book, another one is half-naked, saying: "I have no bread, but I hold fast to Reason." And I too receive no physical sustenance from my studies, but I hold fast to them.

4.31

Hold dear the craft you have learned, take comfort in it, and live out the remainder of your life as one who has entrusted the gods with the entirety of his soul, and who has not established himself as either a tyrant or slave to any other person.

---

6. The Greek word for "abscess" literally means "stands apart."

4.35

They are all short-lived, both those who remember and the remembered.

4.37

Soon you will be dead, and not yet are you of one mind, undisturbed, or without suspicion that you can truly be harmed by external things; nor yet are you gracious in all circumstances; nor are you truly convinced that wisdom and right action are the same thing.

4.39*

Harm to yourself cannot originate in the ruling part of another person, and surely not in some turn of events or alteration of your surroundings. On what, then, does it depend? Upon that part of you which judges what is bad. So prevent this part from making such a decision, and all will be well for you. Even if the body, its closest companion, is cut, burned, covered with dripping sores, or rotted with gangrene; nevertheless, let that part of you which judges all these experiences be at peace, and let it judge as neither good nor bad anything that can happen to the good and bad man alike.

4.41

As Epictetus said, you are a tiny little soul propping up a corpse.

4.43

Eternity is like a river, or even a forceful torrent, of all things that come into being; for at the very moment that a particular thing is seen, it is carried away, and then something else is carried off, and yet another.

4.44

All that happens is just as ordinary and familiar as the rose in springtime and fruit in summer. So are sickness and death, slander and deceit, and whatever else cheers or saddens foolish people.

4.47

If some god told you that you would die tomorrow, or the next day at the latest, you would not consider death on the third day to be anything better than death on the second day, unless you were a wholly base person. And so just the same, do not think that living many years is any better than dying tomorrow.

4.48*

Keep constantly in your mind how many doctors die after a lifetime of wrinkling their brows in thought over the sick; and how many astrologers die after predicting with much ceremony the death of others; and how many philosophers die after exhausting their minds with countless discourses concerning death and immortality; and how many great military men die after killing so many people; and how many tyrants die after exercising their power over the lives of others with an insolent snort, as if they themselves were immortal. And how many entire cities—Helice, Pompeii, Herculaneum,[7] and countless others—have been destroyed. So always keep in mind how short-lived and insignificant human things really are: yesterday a glob of mucous, tomorrow a corpse or a pile of ashes. So pass this brief amount of time in accordance with Nature and dissolve graciously, just as a ripe olive falls to the ground praising both the earth which gave it life and the tree which nourished it.

4.49

Be like the jutting rock against which waves are constantly crashing, and all around it the frothing foam of the waters then settles back down. "Oh, I am so unfortunate that this has happened to me." Not at all, but rather "How fortunate I am that, *even though this has happened to me*, I continue uninjured, neither terrified by the present, nor in fear of the future." So such a thing could happen to anyone, but not just anyone would persevere unharmed. So why is this considered bad fortune rather than good fortune? And do you think something to be wholly unfortunate for a man when it

---

7. Helice was destroyed by an earthquake and tsunami in A.D. 373 (Pausanias 9.30). Pompeii and Herculaneum were destroyed by the eruption of Mount Vesuvius in A.D. 79.

is not even a defect in his nature? And would that which is not contrary to the plan of his nature seem to you a defect in his nature? What then? You have already learned this plan; does what has happened to you prevent you from being just, great-souled,[8] self-controlled, considerate, deliberate, honest, modest, independent, and all other such qualities which, when present, allow us to realize our true nature? For the remainder of your life, whenever anything causes pain for you, make use of this principle: "This is not unfortunate. Indeed, to bear such things nobly is good fortune."

8. The Greek word is *megalopsuchē*, from which English gets the Latinized word "magnanimous."

Book Five

5.1*

Early in the morning, when you are reluctant in your laziness to get up, let this thought be at hand: "I am rising to do the work of a human being." Even though I know this, why am I still resentful if I am going out to do that for which I was born and that for which I was brought into the Cosmos? Or was I created so that I could lie under my covers and keep warm? "But this is more pleasant," you might say. Were you brought into this world simply to feel pleasure, that is, to be acted upon by feelings rather than to act? Have you not considered the plants, the birds, the ants, the spiders, and the bees, all doing their specific work and contributing to the Cosmos, each according to their unique capacities?

And still you do not wish to do the work of a human being? Why are you not hurrying to do what is in accordance with your nature? "But one must also rest." I agree, but Nature has set limits to this, too, just as she has set limits to eating and drinking, and in these you go well beyond the limits. In your actions, however, you stay well within the limits of what you are capable of. You do not love yourself, or else you surely would love your nature and what it intends for you.

5.2

How agreeable it is to drive out and completely let go of every impression that is troublesome or foreign, and be in perfect tranquility!

5.3

Judge every single word or deed that is in accordance with Nature as worthy of you, and do not trouble yourself if reproach or gossip should follow; but rather, if something noble is to be done or said, do not judge yourself unworthy of doing or saying it. For others have their own ruling part and follow their own particular inclinations, to which you should not direct your gaze but continue on your straight path, following both your own personal nature and the Universal Nature, for the paths of both of these are actually one.

5.8

Everyone has heard about Asclepius[9] prescribing horseback riding, or a cold bath, or walking barefoot. In this way, too, has the Nature of the universe prescribed sickness, injury, abandonment, or some other such thing. In the first case,

---

9. The Greek deity of medicine, who was the mythical first physician.

"prescribed" indicates that Asclepius has arranged this medicine to that person because it leads to good health. And also in the second case, whatever should happen has also been arranged for each person because it is in some way conducive to each person's destiny. For we say that things "fall" to us, just as the large square stones in walls or in pyramids "fall" into place, aligning themselves with each other; for the entire universe is one great harmony, and just as the Cosmos is made complete by all material bodies, so too do many unique causes make up the one ordained Cause in Nature. What I mean is understood even by simple people, for even they can say "fate brought this upon him." So one thing has been brought to one person, and another thing has been prescribed to another person. Then let us welcome such things, just as we welcome the prescriptions of Asclepius. In these, too, there is surely much that is harsh, but we nevertheless welcome them in the hope of being cured.

5.9

Do not give up or be disgusted and impatient with yourself if you do not act from right principles in every situation; but, having been driven off course, return again and rejoice if most of your actions are worthy of a human being, and love that to which you are returning. Do not come back to philosophy as a child returns to a harsh schoolmaster but rather as sore-eyed people turn to sponges and egg whites, as one sick man turns to plaster, and another to healing ointments. For to obey the order of the universe is no heroic deed or struggle. But in so doing you will find tranquility.

5.11*

"Toward what end am I now making use of my soul?" Each day question and cross-examine yourself: What is really my own within this very part which people like to call the "ruling part" and which is often that in name only? What kind of soul do I have at this very moment? That of a child? of an adolescent? of a tyrant? of livestock? of a beast?

5.16*

Whatever kind of impressions you receive most often, so too will be your mind, for the soul is dyed with the color of one's impressions. Therefore, color your soul with continuous thoughts like these: wherever there is life, there, too, the good life is possible; there is life in the royal halls, and so even in the royal halls it is possible to live rightly.

5.18

Nothing happens to anyone which that person is unable by nature to endure. The same thing that happens to you can happen to another, and they are steadfast and remain unharmed either because they are ignorant that anything has happened or because they are showing off their so-called greatness of mind. Strange indeed that ignorance and showing off can be stronger than wisdom!

5.20

From one point of view, every human being is closely connected to us; therefore all people must be treated well and tolerated. But from another point of view, insofar as any human stands in the way of actions which are my proper duty, then mankind becomes just another one of all the things which are not my concern, no less than the sun or the wind or a wild animal. Though my action could be hindered by one of these, my motivation and state of mind cannot be hindered, thanks to my ability to step back and adapt to any circumstance. For the mind can convert all that hinders its activity into things which help it, all that checks its work into assistance in that very task, and all that stands in its path into an escort on its journey.

5.27

"Live with the gods," as the saying goes; but what does this mean? He dwells with the gods who constantly shows them a soul that is satisfied with its portion, and which does what its divine spirit wills, that spirit which Zeus gave as a portion of himself to each person, to be their guardian and guide. For this is the Intelligence and Reason of each person.

5.30

The Intelligence of the Whole is shared by all. It has surely made the lower for the sake of the higher, and it has united all things higher for the sake of each other. See for yourself how it has subordinated, arranged, and assigned what is proper to each and has brought the very highest things into agreement with each other.

5.31*

How have you conducted yourself thus far toward the gods, toward your parents, brothers, wife, children, teachers, friends, family, and servants? Consider whether it can be judged of you concerning all of them, that "he never said or did anything harmful."[10]

Recall to your mind all that you have passed through and all that you have been able to endure; and that the story of your life will soon come to an end, and your duty will be accomplished. Recall, too, all the beautiful things you have seen and how many pleasures and pains you have seen through, how many honors you have turned away from, and how much unkindness you have repaid with kindness.

---

10. The reference is to Homer's *Odyssey*, 4.690. Penelope, wife of Odysseus, is telling her suitors about her husband, Odysseus, who has been gone for many years and is thought dead.

5.33

In no time at all you will be ashes, a skeleton, or perhaps just a name—or not even a name, for a name is just an empty sound or a faint echo. The things which are valued in this life are empty, rotten, petty, like the snapping of dogs or children's games: now laughing, now crying. But we see that trust, modesty before the gods, justice, and truth have, in the poet's words, "fled to Olympus, far away from the wide expanse of earth."[11] What is it, then, which still holds you here, if indeed the objects of perception are constantly changing and never standing still, and if your senses are dull and easily misled, and if the soul itself is merely an exhalation from the blood,[12] and if having a good reputation in the midst of all this is an empty thing? What then? Why aren't you calmly awaiting death, whether it be either extinction or some other kind of change? And until this time comes, what should we do? What else but to honor and praise the gods, to act well toward others, practicing tolerance and self-restraint; since all that lies within the limits of mere flesh and spirit is neither yours nor in your power?

---

11. Hesiod, *Works and Days,* lines 197 and following, describes the fate of the fallen race of men, where the last of the gods "will go from the wide-pathed earth and forsake mankind to join the company of the deathless gods: and bitter sorrows will be left for mortal men, and there will be no help against evil."

12. This is one ancient theory of the nature of the soul. See Heraclitus fr. 12 and Aristotle *De Anima* 405a25.

5.34

It is always within your power to make life flow favorably if you can choose the right path, that is, if you can think and act rightly.[13] Both the gods and humans (who are creatures instilled with Reason) have these characteristics in common: the ability not to be hindered by externals, and to understand that the Good consists in the cultivation of a just attitude and just actions, and to limit one's desire according to this.

5.37

"There was a time, long past, when fate was kind to me."[14] But the truly fortunate person has created his own good fortune through good habits of the soul, good intentions, and good actions.

---

13. The Greek word for "rightly," *hodō*, is derived from the word *hodos*, meaning "road" or "path."
14. A common tragic lament.

Book Six

❖

6.2

Whether you are shivering with cold or too hot, sleepy or wide awake, spoken well of or badly, dying, or doing anything else, do not let it interfere with doing what is right. For whatever causes us to die is also one of life's processes. Even for this, nothing more is required of us than to accomplish well the task at hand.

6.3

Always look to what is inside. Never allow the true essence and worth of a thing to escape you.

6.6

The noblest way of taking revenge on others is by refusing to become like them.

6.7

Take pleasure and rest in one thing only: making your way from one communal duty to another, always remembering god.

6.8

The governing part is that which rouses itself and adapts itself; it makes itself into whatever it wishes, and whatever may happen to the governing part, it makes all circumstances appear to be in accordance with its wishes.

6.10

Either everything is a confused gathering and scattering of atoms, or else it is all a great unity and design. If the former, why am I so eager to go on living in such a swirling chaos? Why should I care about anything but how I will finally "return to the soil"?[15] and why am I disturbed? For whatever I do, this scattering will come upon me as well. But if it is the other alternative, then I am reverent, I am calm; I place my trust in that which governs all things.

6.11

Whenever you are forced by circumstances to be disturbed in some way, quickly return to yourself, and do not lose your footing any longer than is absolutely necessary; for you will have more control over your internal harmony by continually returning to it.

---

15. Homer, *Iliad,* 7.97–100. Menelaus berates his companions when no one displays the courage to fight Hector, an almost certain death.

6.14*

Most things which are valued by the bulk of humanity fall into the most general category of things that are held together either by natural cohesion, such as stones and wood, or by a principle of natural growth, like vines and figs. But those things which are valued by more thoughtful people can be grouped among those held together by a principle of soul, such as flocks, herds, or the mere possession of slaves. And things which are valued by still more educated people are held together by a rational soul—not according to Reason in itself but like the knowledge of a master craftsman or someone who is skilled in some other way. But the person who prizes the rational and social soul above all things, protects its movements and cooperates with other reasoning people toward this end.

6.16

To absorb air as plants do should not be valued much, nor the act of respiration, which we share with cattle and wild animals, nor the act of being affected by impressions, nor to be manipulated by our impulses like a marionette, nor to live in herds, nor to consume nutriment, for this last one is no better than to value the expelling of that nutriment.

What then should we value? The clapping of hands? Surely not. And not the clapping of tongues either, for praise by the masses is nothing other than this. So now you have done away with fame as well. What then remains to be valued? I believe it is this: to move and be restrained in accordance with how we are made and what we are made for, toward which end both our concerns and our arts lead (for indeed every art or craft aims at this, in order that whatever it constructs be well suited for its proper task, for which it has been made. And this is the aim of the gardener who cares for the vine, the horse trainer, and the breeder of dogs). And what about the upbringing and education of children? What end do these arts seek? Surely what is honorable. And if you are in possession of this, nothing else will you seek for yourself. Will you not then cease to value all of those other things? For otherwise you would not be free, self-sufficient, or unaffected but compelled to envy, jealousy, and suspicion of those who possess what you want.

In sum, such a person will necessarily be in complete confusion who feels the need for any of those things, and will even find fault with the gods. But through reverence for one's own capacity for thought one can be acceptable to oneself, accommodating to other people, and a companion to the gods, namely by praising whatever they have assigned and ordered.

6.19

If something is difficult for you to accomplish, do not then think it impossible for any human being; rather, if it is humanly possible and corresponds to human nature, know that it is attainable by you as well.

6.21*

If someone is able to show me that what I think or do is not right, I will happily change, for I seek the truth, by which no one ever was truly harmed. Harmed is the person who continues in his self-deception and ignorance.

6.27

How cruel not to allow people to pursue what appears proper and beneficial to them. Yet in a sense you prevent them from doing just this when you are irritated at their mistake; for they are certainly drawn toward what seems proper and beneficial to them. "But they are mistaken," you might say. Then teach and enlighten them, but don't be irritated.

6.29

It is disgraceful for the soul to fail in this lifetime, even before the body does.

6.31*

Regain your senses, call yourself back, and once again wake up. Now that you realize that only dreams were troubling you, view this "reality" as you view your dreams.

6.33

It is not contrary to Nature for the hand or the foot to suffer, so long as the foot does the work of the foot, and the hand does the work of the hand. Neither is the suffering of a person contrary to Nature, so long as he is doing the proper work of the human being. If it is not contrary to Nature, then it is not an evil to the person.

6.35

Haven't you seen how even lowly craftsmen accommodate laymen to a certain point but all the time hold fast to the principle of their craft and never allow themselves to abandon it? Isn't it strange, then, that a craftsman or a doctor should respect the principles of their particular specialty more than a man does his own Reason, which he in fact shares with the gods?

6.36

Asia and Europe: tiny corners of the Cosmos. Every sea: a mere drop. Mount Athos: a lump of dirt. The present moment is the smallest point in eternity. All is microscopic, changeable, disappearing. All things come from that faraway place, either originating directly from that governing part which is common to all or else following from it as consequences. So even the gaping jaws of the lion, deadly poison, and all harmful things like thorns or an oozing bog are products of that awesome and noble source. Do not imagine these things to be alien to that which you revere, but turn your Reason to the source of all things.[16]

6.37

The person who truly sees the present has already seen everything—all that has come from eternity and all that will happen in the infinite future—for all things are of one ancestry and likeness.

6.38

Consider often the connection of all things in the Cosmos and their relationship with each other. For in a way all things are mutually intertwined, and thus according to this there is a natural inclination, or love, that links everything together. For things follow another by reason of their attunement, the common spirit that breathes through them, and the unity of all being.

6.40*

Every tool, instrument, or vessel is good if it performs well that function for which it was made; and yet, in such cases, the maker is external to it. But for those creatures who are made by Nature, the power that made them is within and

---

16. The bog has been understood to represent our normal state of existence, as opposed to the clarity and purity of the starry sky.

remains there. Because of this, you must honor that power all the more and understand that if you conduct yourself and live your life in accordance with Nature's will, then everything will be in accordance with your Intelligence.

6.44

If the gods have made decisions concerning me, in particular what must happen to me, no doubt they have made good decisions, for not easily could one conceive of a god who is lacking in wisdom. And what reason would he have for wanting to harm me? What benefit could there be to the Whole, for which they care most of all? But if they have not made decisions concerning me alone but have done so concerning the Whole, then I am obliged to welcome and be content with all that happens to me according to this sequence of natural events. If, however, they make no decisions—blasphemous to think, or else let us no longer sacrifice, pray, swear by them, or do any of the other things which we do in the belief that they are present and live among us—if it is indeed the case that they do not make decisions concerning my interests, it nevertheless remains within *my* power to make decisions concerning myself. My search is for what is beneficial. The benefit for each is in accordance with how they are made and their specific nature, and my nature pertains both to Reason and to society. My city is Rome, insofar as I am Antoninus; but insofar as I am a human being, my city is the Cosmos. Therefore all that benefits these cities is alone my good.

6.48

Whenever you want to cheer yourself up, consider the good qualities of your companions, for example, the energy of one, the modesty of another, the generosity of yet another, and some other quality of another; for nothing cheers the heart as much as the images of excellence reflected in the character of our companions, all brought before us as fully as possible. Therefore, keep these images ready at hand.

6.49

Are you discontented because you weigh only as much as you do and not three hundred pounds? In the same way, are you upset because you can live only so many years and not more? Therefore, just as you are satisfied with the amount of bulk that has been assigned to you, so too with your lifetime.

6.51

The person who loves reputation supposes that his own good depends on the activities of others; the lover of pleasure finds his own good in being affected by his emotions. But the person who has Intelligence understands the good to be in his own actions.

Book Seven

7.48*

When studying mankind, it is necessary to examine earthly matters as if from above, looking down upon herds, armies, farms, unions and separations, births and deaths, the noisy courtrooms and deserted places, foreign peoples of all kinds, celebrations, mournings, marketplaces—all as a great mixture and a harmonious order that is made from opposites.

7.55*

Do not look around you to what guides others but look straight at this: Where is Nature leading you? By this I mean both the nature of the Whole which acts upon you, and your own nature which requires action by you. But everyone must do what is in accordance with their constitution, and all other parts of the person have been constituted for the sake of the rational part, just as in every other case the lower exist for the sake of the higher. But rational beings have been made for the sake of each other.

7.57

Whatever should happen to you, love that alone, for it has been spun for you by the Fates themselves.[17] Could anything be more fitting?

7.59

Turn your attention within, for the fountain of all that is good lies within, and it is always ready to pour forth, if you continually delve in.

7.65

See that you never feel toward the inhumane what they feel toward humankind.

7.69

Fulfillment of one's character is the attainment of this: to live each day as if it were the last; to be neither agitated nor numb; and never to act with pretense.

7.71

It is ridiculous to renounce the wickedness of others, which is impossible, rather than renounce one's own wickedness, which *is* possible.

---

17. The Greeks and Romans typically depicted the Fates as spinning time and destiny on a yarn wheel.

7.73

When you have done a good act and another has fared well by it, why seek a third reward besides these, as fools do, be it the reputation for having done a good act or getting something in return?

Book Eight

❧

8.2

For every action ask yourself: "How does this relate to me? Will I regret it? In a short time, I will be dead, and all things will be gone. What more, then, do I seek, if my present work befits an intelligent and communal being, one who is governed by the same law as the gods?"

8.4

Do what you will. Even if you tear yourself apart, they will continue doing the same things.

8.8

No time to read or study. But it *is* possible to restrain my pride; it *is* possible to rise above pleasures and pains; it *is* possible to rise above reputation; it *is* possible not only *not* to be angry with the insensitive and ungrateful but even to care for them.

8.12

Whenever you are annoyed at waking up from sleep, remember that performing communal duties is in accord with your makeup and with human nature but that you share sleeping even with unreasoning animals. That which is in accordance with the nature of each, then, is more closely related, suitable by nature, and even more pleasurable.

8.19

Each thing has come into existence for a specific purpose, like a horse or a grapevine. Even the sun would say: "I exist for a purpose," and also the other gods.[18] What, then, is your purpose? To feel pleasure? See if the mind will allow such a thought.

8.26

A man's joy is in doing that which is specifically human. And what is specifically human is a benevolent disposition toward his own kind, seeing beyond the movements of the senses, rightly discerning the persuasive pictures offered by the imagination, and contemplating the nature of the Whole and its works.

---

18. According to many branches of ancient philosophy, the planets, stars, and heavenly bodies are considered to be gods and divine, as much as the personified deities.

8.29

Master your impressions by continually saying this to yourself: "Now it is in my power that within this soul there be no wickedness, appetite, nor any agitation at all. But, seeing things for what they truly are, I will make use of each one according to its real worth." Remember this power that you have been given by Nature.

8.32

It is necessary to construct one's life one action at a time and be content if each of these actions accomplishes its own task as far as possible. There is not a single person who can hinder you so as to prevent this. "But something external will stand in my way." There is no such thing when it comes to acting justly, with self-restraint and understanding. "But perhaps some other activity will be hindered." Nevertheless, by gracefully accepting the obstacle and by thoughtfully turning toward that which has been given to you, immediately another action will take its place, one which fully corresponds to the synthesis that we are speaking of.

8.33

Receive without conceit; release without a struggle.

8.45

Pick me up and place me back down wherever you wish, for even there I will keep my divine spirit beneficent, that is, sufficient in itself, if it remains well disposed and acts in accordance with its nature. Is any particular circumstance worthy of my soul becoming evil on account of it or made base, craving, enslaved, frightened? Can you think of anything that justifies becoming like this?

8.46

Nothing can happen to a human being which is not a human incident, that is, proper to humans. Nor can anything happen to an ox which is not proper to an ox, nor to a vine which is not proper to a vine, nor to a stone which is not proper to a stone. So if whatever happens to each one of these is accustomed and natural, why are you troubled? For the common Nature that we all share has not brought you anything unbearable.

8.48

Remember that the ruling part of the self becomes unconquerable when it collects itself and is contented with itself, doing nothing it does not will, even if the stand it takes is unreasonable. How much more, then, when it judges *with* reason and considers all sides of a matter? Thus the mind which is free from disturbance is a citadel of refuge, for humans have nothing stronger in which they can find refuge and remain uncaptured. Whoever has not seen this is ignorant; whoever has seen this and does not seek refuge is doomed.

8.49

Do not tell yourself more than your impressions announce. You have been told that someone speaks badly of you. This is what you have been told; you have not seen that you are injured by this. I see that this child is sick; this is all that I see. I do not see that the child is in danger. In this way, then, always remain with your original impressions. Add nothing else from within yourself, and nothing will happen to you; or, rather, add to them only as one would who truly knows what happens within the universal order of the Cosmos.

8.51*

Do not be sloppy in your actions; in conversation, do not be dragged into confusion; and do not allow your thoughts to wander aimlessly. Do not allow your soul either to contract or inflate; and in your external life, do not be overly busy. "But they kill us, hack us to pieces, and pursue us with curses." What does any of this have to do with keeping your thought pure, composed, restrained, and just? It is as if someone standing by a fountain of pure and sweet water were to yell curses at it, yet the fountain never stops bubbling with fresh water. Even if you should hurl mud or even throw shit into it, the water will quickly disperse it and wash it away, and in no way be defiled. How, then, can you have such a fountain within yourself? By guarding your freedom each and every hour with kindness, simplicity, and self-respect.

8.53*

Do you desire to be praised by a man who curses himself three times every hour? Do you desire to gain the approval of people who do not even approve of themselves?

8.57

The sun seems to pour itself down, and pours itself in every direction, but it is not emptied. For this pouring is an extension, and its rays are so named because of their extension. You can observe this if you watch sunlight shining through some narrow crack in a dark room. It extends itself in a straight line until it encounters some solid body which stops its extension. There the light rests, and it does not move or fall off.

This is how the pouring and diffusion of the mind must be, for it is not a pouring *out*, but rather an extension of itself; and it should not make a violent or angry impact upon whatever stands in its way; nor should it simply fall away, but rather it should stand firm and illuminate whatever receives it. Whatever does not accept it and help it on its way only deprives itself of the light.

8.59

Humans have come into being for the sake of each other; so teach them or learn to bear them.

Book Nine

9.3*

Do not see death as a hindrance, but accept it, since even death is something that Nature wishes. For just like youth, old age, growth, maturity, the growing of teeth, beard, and gray hair, conception, pregnancy and birth, and all the other activities of Nature which the seasons of life bring—so too is dissolution a natural process. It therefore corresponds to what we are as beings possessed of Reason not to be rash, violent, or arrogant toward death but to await it as one of Nature's processes. And just as you await the time when the child comes forth from your wife's womb, in the same way you should welcome the hour when your soul emerges from its shell.

9.4

He who acts wrongly harms himself. If a person commits an injustice, he acts badly toward himself, thus making himself bad.

9.5

Very often an unjust act is done by *not* doing something, not only by doing something.

9.8

One animating principle is distributed among all unreasoning creatures, and one Mind is portioned out among reasoning creatures. In the same way, there is one Earth that is the source of all earthly things, and there is one light and one air for us who see and live.

9.9*

All beings which participate in something common to them tend toward each other. The earthly tends toward the earth; all that is liquid runs together; airy things are so similar that they must be held apart by force; fire rises because of its elemental nature, but will also combine through combustion with material that is easily ignited from lack of moisture.

In a similar way, all that naturally shares in a common mind tends toward what is related to it, for insofar as this type of commonality is superior to the rest, the more readily will it join and mix with its own kind. Even among creatures without reason there arose hives, flocks, the care of newborns, and what appears to be loving-care in general, for even in them there was a vital spirit, and a unifying tendency could be discovered in them to a higher degree than in plants, stones, or trees. Among creatures possessing reason there arose communities, households, gatherings, and treaties and truces during disputes. Among still higher beings, even those who were separated in some way, there was a unity like that of the heavenly bodies.

But what happens now? These beings alone have forgotten their natural zeal to come together; only among them is this phenomenon missing. But they are nevertheless overtaken, though they flee, for Nature is strong. Watch carefully and you will see: for sooner would you see earthly things defying gravity than human beings completely severed from each other.

9.10

Man, god, and the Cosmos all bear fruit, each in their proper time. What does it matter that the phrase "bear fruit" is usually used referring only to the vine and similar things? Reason too bears fruit, both for itself and for others, and it produces from itself what is like itself.

9.11

If you can, teach others to become better; if you cannot, then remember that the power to be kind has been given to you for this purpose. Even the gods care for such people and help them to gain health, wealth, and reputation, so helpful are they. Such kindness is also in your power, or tell me, who is there to prevent you?

9.13

Today I escaped all difficulty; or rather, I have *cast out* all difficulty, for difficulty is not external, but rooted in my judgments.

9.16

Just as excellence and evil do not reside in being acted upon but rather in acting, so it is with the good and evil of any reasoning communal being.

9.17

For the stone that has been thrown into the air, it is no evil to come down; nor is it a good to have been tossed up.

9.23

Just as you yourself play an essential role in the social body, so should each of your actions help to perfect a communal life. Therefore, any action of yours which does not bear some direct or indirect relation to this common goal will fragment your life, disrupting its unity and creating internal strife, just like the person in the public assembly who, for his own interests, stands apart from the community.

9.27*

Whenever someone blames or hates you, or if anyone should express such sentiments, go directly to their souls, pass into them, and see who they really are. You will then see that you do not have to trouble yourself about what such people may think of you. However, you must be kind to them, for they too are your natural friends.

9.32

Many of the superfluous things which trouble you are products of your own judgment, and you have the power to strip them away and be free of them. If you do this, immediately you will create a vast expanse for yourself, grasping with your mind the whole Cosmos, contemplating both the endless movement of time and the rapidly changing nature of all that exists. How brief the interval between birth and death; how wide the expanse of time before birth, as infinite as that after death.

9.34

See the kind of internal ruler they have, to what they give their attention, and what things such people love and honor! Learn to look into their naked souls. How great they suppose they are, when they believe that by blaming they do harm and that by praising they help.

9.40

Either the gods have power or they do not. If they do not, why do you pray? But if they do have power, why aren't you praying that they give you the power not to fear, crave, or be troubled by a thing, rather than praying to have that thing or not have it? For if the gods can work with us, then surely they can work with us toward this end. Then you might say, "But the gods have already given me this power." Well then, isn't it a better thing freely to make use of the gifts you have, instead of slavishly worrying about what is not in your control? Who has told you that the gods do not also assist us with what is *within* our power?

Begin to pray in the following way, and you will see. Someone else may pray: "How may I possess that woman?" But you should pray: "How may I not lust after that woman?" Someone else prays: "How can I be rid of him?" But you: "How can I not wish to be rid of him?" Another: "How may I not lose my little child?" But you: "How may I not dread the loss of my child?" Turn your prayers around entirely, and see what happens.

9.42

When you see the shameless behavior of someone, immediately ask yourself: Is it possible for there to be no shameless people in the world? Impossible, so do not ask for what is impossible, for this person, too, is one of those shameless people who are destined to exist in the world. Let this thought be at hand also for the villain, the liar, and everyone who has gone astray. For when you remember that this type of person cannot help but exist, you will be kinder toward each and every one of them.

It is also useful immediately to consider this: what power has Nature given us for dealing with such people? For She has given us kindness as an antidote for the arrogant, and other faculties for dealing with other difficulties. In a word, it is in your power to teach whoever has lost his way, and everyone who is in error is so in relation to his true goal and has gone astray from that goal. And how has this harmed you? For you will discover that not one of those who have made you angry has done anything which makes your mind worse, and it is there, in your understanding, that all evil and harm have their dwelling.

What is evil or even strange about an ignorant person doing ignorant things? Rather, see to it that you aren't to blame for not anticipating that this person would be in error; remember that you possess the resources of Reason, which will allow you to see that this person will most likely be mistaken, and yet you have forgotten, and so you are amazed when he does so.

But, most important, whenever you accuse someone of being a liar or unkind, turn inward to yourself, for the fault clearly lies with you, either because you trusted that such a person would keep his word or because, once you had given a favor, you did not do this unconditionally and you forgot that you received the entire fruit of your action in that moment. For what more do you want, dear man, once you have done something good? Do you want some additional compensation? Does the eye demand wages for seeing or the feet for walking? Just as these were made for something and, in accomplishing their task, gain what is truly theirs, so too is man naturally a doer of good actions, and when he has done such an action, he has accomplished what he was made for and receives what is truly his.

Book Ten

※

10.6*

Whatever one's theory of the universe, this must be established first of all: I am a part of the Whole which is governed by Nature. Second: I have some sort of allegiance toward those parts of the Whole which are like me. For if I remember these two things, I will not be discontented by anything that has been assigned to me by the Whole, since I am a part of it, for nothing which benefits the Whole is truly harmful to a part because the Whole does not contain anything that is not beneficial to itself. While all natural things possess this feature, the universe has this in addition: it cannot be compelled by some external cause to generate something harmful to itself.

10.11

How is it that all things change, one into another? Acquire a contemplative way of investigating this question, and continually apply yourself to this practice. Nothing so promotes greatness of mind. Such a person has shed the burden of his body and, having realized that soon he must leave all people and things behind, devotes himself entirely to justice in what he can accomplish and to the will of Universal Nature in all other circumstances. To whatever people say, think, or do concerning him, he pays no mind but is satisfied with these two things: justly performing his present actions and welcoming his present circumstance. He has eagerly put aside all preoccupation with unnecessary matters, and desires nothing but to pursue a straight path according to Universal Law, for in so doing he follows god.

10.15

Your life is almost over. Live as though you were on an isolated mountaintop, for it makes no difference where someone is, if they can live anywhere in the world as a citizen of the greater human community. Let them see, let men come to know a true man, one who lives according to Nature. If they cannot bear him, let them kill him, for this would be better for him than to live as they live.

10.16

Stop philosophizing about what a good man is and be one.

10.23

Let it always be clear to you that this land is like any other and that everything is the same here as it would be on the summit of a mountain or by the sea or wherever you wish. For you will discover exactly what Plato says: "walling himself in upon a mountain and living off the milk of his flock."[19]

10.25

Whoever flees his master is a fugitive, and Universal Law, too, is a master. Therefore, whoever goes against Law is also a fugitive. Similarly, giving way to anger and fear is to wish that things past, present, or future not exist which are assigned by the Governor of all things, which is Universal Law ordering what is given to each person. Therefore, whoever gives in to fear, pain, or anger is a fugitive.

10.27

Continually be mindful of how everything that happens now has also happened in previous times and will happen in the future. And place before your eyes all the dramas and stage-sets, which you have learned either from experience or from older accounts, such as the royal court of Hadrian, of Antoninus, of Philip, Alexander, and Croesus—for those were the same dramas as we see now; only the actors are different.

---

19. Marcus reminds himself of a passage in Plato's *Theaetetus* (174 d–e), during a discussion in which the benefits of land ownership are contrasted with the life of the philosopher, who, by owning nothing, in fact "owns" the entire world.

10.29

For each thing you do, stop and ask yourself if death is to be feared because it deprives you of this.

10.30

Whenever you notice someone else going astray, immediately turn and examine how you yourself have gone astray, for example, esteeming money, pleasure, reputation, or something else, as if it were the highest good. Examine yourself in this way and you will quickly forget your anger. Then, consider that the person who has gone astray has been compelled to do so, for what else could he do? But if you are able, remove that in him which is subject to compulsion.

10.34

For a person who has been "stung" by true principles of action, even the briefest and most common saying is enough to rid oneself of pain and fear. For example:

As the wind scatters leaves upon the earth,
such is the race of men.[20]

---

20. In Marcus' time, the epic poetry of Homer and Virgil comprised not only a literary but also a philosophical and religious education. This passage, and the quotes that follow, paraphrase Homer's *Iliad*, 6.146-9.

Your children, too, are "leaves"; so are those who loyally applaud and praise you, as well as those who curse you, reproach you in secret, and mock you. Leaves, too, are those who will carry on a person's reputation; for all these things "grow in the springtime," and then the wind casts them down, and "the forest produces others in place of them." A short life is common to all, yet you avoid and pursue things as though you will live forever. In a little while you, too, will close your eyes, and soon after that another will mourn the person who carried your coffin.

10.38

Remember that your puppet-strings are pulled by what is hidden within. This is the source of activity, this is the source of life, this—if it must be said—is man. Never confuse it with the flesh that surrounds it like a vessel or with your limbs and organs, for these are all "tools" which have been attached to you.[21] They are like an axe or any other tool, the only difference being that they are permanently attached. These "tools" are of no more use without the cause which manipulates and restrains them than the loom without the weaver, the pen without the writer, or the whip without the charioteer.

---

21. Marcus here points out the separate but related meanings of the Greek word *organon*, "tool," which we retain in English as "organ."

Book Eleven

11.1

Characteristics which are unique to the reasoning soul: it truly sees itself, shapes itself, and makes itself into whatever it wills. It harvests the fruit which it bears (whereas the fruits of plants or the hunt are gathered by others). It accomplishes its goal, whenever the limit of its life may come. If something should hinder it, its entire action is not therefore incomplete, as in a dance or play or something of the sort. Rather, in every aspect, and at whatever point it is overcome, it fully accomplishes what it had set out to do, so that it can say: "I possess what is truly my own."

Moreover, the reasoning soul penetrates the whole Cosmos as well as the surrounding void, learning its shape, extending itself into the infinity of the ages, embracing and understanding the cyclic rebirth of the universe. It perceives that those who come after us will see nothing new and that those who came before did not see anything more; but that, in a sense, the man of forty, if he has any real understanding at all, has seen all that has happened and all that will happen within the pattern that shapes all things.

Another attribute unique to the reasoning soul is love of one's neighbor, love of truth, self-respect, and honoring nothing above the soul itself. This is also an attribute of law, for in this sense, there is no difference between right reason and the principle of justice.

11.4

"Are my actions appropriate for a communal being? If so, I have my reward." Keep this thought always at hand, and never cease.

11.5

To what craft do you devote yourself? Simply to be good. But how can this come about except from obedience to the principles of thought concerning both Nature as a whole and the specific makeup of the human being?

11.6*

Tragic plays were first performed as reminders of how things often come to pass, that it is in accordance with Nature that things happen that way, and that the suffering that pleases you on the stage should not cause you distress on the Great Stage. For you see that things must happen in a certain way, and even those who cry "O Cithaeron"[22] are able to endure them.

11.7

What could be clearer? No other life is more appropriate for the practice of philosophy than that life which you now happen to be living.

11.8*

A tree branch that is cut off from its nearest neighboring branch cannot help but be cut off from the entire tree. In the same way, one man when severed from another man is cut off from the whole community. But whereas the branch is severed by someone or something else, man severs *himself* from his neighbor by hating him and turning away from him, not realizing that he simultaneously separates himself from the whole of society.

11.9

Those who try to hinder you as you move forward according to right reason do not have the power to turn you away from sound actions. Neither should you allow them to drive away

---

22. Sophocles, *Oedipus Rex*, 1391. Oedipus, upon discovering his tragic fate, laments that Cithaeron, the sacred mountain upon which he was abandoned as an infant, allowed him to live.

the benevolent disposition that you have toward them. So guard yourself equally in these two circumstances: not only firmness in your judgments and actions but also gentleness with those who try to hinder or annoy you in some other way. For to be angry with them is weakness, just as much as it is weakness to abandon your practices or to yield because of fear. For both are deserters of their post: the trembling coward, as well as he who is alienated from a natural kinsman and friend.

11.11

They do not come to you, those things whose pursuit or avoidance disturbs you, but in a sense, you go toward them. Therefore let your judgments about them be untroubled and they will not trouble you, and you will not be seen pursuing or avoiding them.

11.15

How worthless and deceitful is the person who says: "I have decided to be straightforward in my dealings with you." What are you doing, my good man? There is no need to say this in advance. It will soon show itself; it might as well be written on one's forehead. The voice has the power to shine at once through the eyes, just as the beloved immediately knows everything from the mere glance of the lover. The good and straightforward person should resemble one who stinks of goat, in the sense that whoever comes close will immediately sense him, whether they want to or not. But a contrived simplicity is like a dagger. Nothing is more shameful than the wolf's friendship; avoid this most of all. The good, simple, and kind person has all these qualities in the eyes, and no one can fail to see it.

11.18*

Nine principles to remember
when dealing with those who offend you

First, consider exactly what my relation toward them is, and that we have come into being for each other. To put it another way, I was born to be their protector, just like a ram for the flock or a bull for the herd. Going back further still, if it is not all simply atoms, then Nature orders all things. And if this is so, then the lower exist for the higher, and the higher for each other.

Second, consider what sort they are while at the dinner table, in bed, and so on; especially what kinds of compulsions they are subject to because of their opinions and with what arrogance they act as they do.

Third, that if in fact they are acting rightly, we should not be angry with them; but if they do not act rightly, they clearly do so involuntarily and in ignorance, for only unwillingly does the soul lack the ability to be properly disposed toward each person, just as the soul unwillingly lacks the truth. Notice how all people resent being called unjust, ignorant, greedy, or generally mistaken about their neighbors.

The Essential Marcus Aurelius

Fourth, remember that you yourself are often mistaken, and so you are just like them; also that, even if you manage to refrain from doing some wrongs, you nevertheless have it in you to do such things, were it not for the fact that fear, thirst for reputation, or some other unworthy motive keeps you from doing what they do.

Fifth, that you are not even sure that they do wrong, for many actions are done within a certain context, and in general, one must know many things before correctly judging the actions of another.

Sixth, whenever you are excessively disturbed or even suffering, remember that human life lasts only a moment and that in a short time we will all be laid out for burial.

Seventh, that it is not the actions of others that trouble us (for those actions are controlled by *their* governing part) but rather it is our own judgments. Therefore remove these judgments and resolve to let go of your judgment that someone's action is terrible, and your anger is already gone. How do you let go? By realizing that such actions are not shameful to *you*.

Eighth, that anger and the sorrow it produces are far more harmful than the things that make us angry.

Ninth, that kindness is unconquerable, so long as it is without flattery or hypocrisy. For what can the most insolent man do to you, if you continue to be kind to him and, *if* you have the chance, gently advise and calmly show him what is right at the very moment he is trying to harm you, saying: "No, my son. We were born for something else. I am certainly not harmed, but you bring harm to yourself"? And point this out to him tactfully and from a universal perspective, that not even bees act that way or any creature that is communal by nature. But you must not do this with sarcasm or reproach but lovingly and without anger in your soul; not as though you were teaching and wanted bystanders to admire you; but even if others are present, address him as if you were alone together.

Remember these nine basic precepts, receiving them as gifts from the Muses; and in so doing, begin at last to live as a human being while you are still living. And be on your guard equally against flattery and anger toward others, for both are harmful and detrimental to community. Also, let this principle be present in your mind whenever you are angry: that anger is in no way manly but rather that gentleness and calm, insofar as they are the most faulty human qualities, are also most befitting of a man. It is this person who has strength, nerve, and courage, not a person who is angry and dissatisfied, for the closer one is to being unaffected, the closer he is to real power; and just as excessive sorrow is a mark of weakness, so is anger, for whoever gives in to these has not merely been wounded, but he has surrendered to his wounds.

And, if you so wish, receive a tenth gift from the leader of the Muses, Apollo: that it is insanity to expect that bad people not do bad things, for this is to aim at what is impossible.

Also, that by allowing such people to act in that way toward others, while demanding that they not wrong you, you are being unjust and tyrannical.

11.24

During their festivals, the Spartans would place the seats for their guests in the shade and then sit themselves down wherever there was room.

11.26

The Epicureans in their writings established this precept: always keep in your mind one of those ancients who practiced virtue.

11.27

The Pythagoreans say this: at dawn, behold the starry heavens, so that we may remind ourselves of those beings that are always in accord with each other and always performing their function; and also so that we remember their order, purity, and nakedness, for a star needs no veil.

11.29

In the disciplines of writing and recitation, you cannot make new rules if you have not first learned how to follow rules. Even more so with living.

Book Twelve

12.1

The goal that you hope you will one day arrive at after a long and roundabout journey you are able to possess right now, if only you do not deny it to yourself. That is, if you can let go of the past, entrust the future to Providence and redirect the present according to justice and the sacred. To the sacred, so that you welcome what has been given to you, for Nature has brought this to you, and you to it; and to justice, in order that you may speak the truth freely and without distortion, and that you may act in accordance with what is lawful and right. Do not allow yourself to be hindered by the harmful actions, judgments, or the words of another, or by the sensations of the flesh which has formed itself around you. Let the body take care of those. But if, when you have come to the end, having let go of all other things, you honor only your guiding part and the divinity that is within you, and you do not fear ceasing to live so much as you fear never having begun to live in accordance with Nature—then you will be a man who is worthy of the Cosmos that created you; and you will cease to live like a stranger in your own land, that is, surprised at unexpected everyday occurrences and wholly distracted by this and that.

12.3

You are composed of three parts: body, vital spirit, and mind. The first two belong to you only insofar as you are obliged to take care of them, but only the third, mind, is truly yours. Therefore, if you can separate yourself (your mind, that is) from all that others do or say and all that you yourself have done or said, all that worries you about the future, all that belongs to the encompassing body which is attached to you without your consent, and all that the external rotation of the heavens causes to whirl around and around, so that the power of mind within you, freed from its fate, can live for itself without pollution or stain, all the while doing what is just, wishing for nothing more than what happens, and speaking the truth. If, I say, you can separate this ruling part from all that is attached to it through the senses, and all that will happen and has already happened, you will make yourself like the sphere of Empedocles: "Completely whole, rejoicing in its solitude." And if you take care to live only what can truly be called life, that is, the present moment, you will be able to spend the time that remains until death undisturbed, with kindness and obedience to the divine spirit within.

12.4*

I have often been amazed at how every person loves himself more than he loves others yet places less value on his own judgment of himself than on the judgments of others concerning him. If a god or some wise teacher were to stand next to him and order him not to think or conceive of anything without at the same time speaking it for all to hear, he would not be able to endure it even for a single day. This shows us that what others think of us counts more for us than our own estimation of ourselves.

12.9

In the application of principles, you must be like the boxer, not the gladiator, for the latter must put down and take up his weapon, while the boxer has his hand with him always and need only make a fist.

12.11

What an exalted position of power and authority is given to man: to do only what the god approves and to welcome all that the god assigns him.

12.12

Never place blame upon the gods, for they do not err, either willingly or unwillingly. Nor should you blame people, for they do not err willingly. Therefore, blame no one.

12.13

How ridiculous, what a stranger in his own land, is the person who is surprised by anything that happens in life.

12.14

Either predetermined necessity and unalterable cosmic order, or a gracious providence, or a chaotic ungoverned mixture. If a predetermined necessity, why do you resist? If it is a gracious Providence that can hear our prayers, then make yourself worthy of divine assistance. If a chaotic ungoverned mixture, be satisfied that in the midst of this storm, you have within yourself a mind whose nature it is to govern and command. So even if the storm should carry you off, let it carry off your flesh, your vital breath, and the rest, for it will not take your mind.

12.21

Consider that before long you will be nobody and nowhere; nor will even one of the things you now see continue to exist. Nor even one of those who now live. For it is the nature of all things to change, to move, and to perish so that another may come to be in their place.

12.22

Consider that everything is what it is according to how you judge it and that your judgment is within your power. Therefore remove the judgment whenever you wish, just like a sailor who has come round the shoreline to the calm waters of a sheltered bay.

12.25

Cast out your judgments and you will be saved. Who, then, prevents you from doing this?

12.26

Whenever you are troubled by anything, you have forgotten. You have forgotten that all things happen in accordance with the Nature of the Whole; you have forgotten that the mistake of another is not your concern; you have also forgotten that everything that happens always happens in this way, has always happened, will happen again, and now happens everywhere; you have forgotten how great the kinship is between one man and the whole of mankind—not simply in blood and parentage but as a Community of the Mind. You have also forgotten that each mind is a god which has come down from above. You have forgotten that nothing belongs to anyone, but even a person's child, body, and breath all come from that source. You have forgotten that all this is merely what we judge it to be, and that each person only lives the present life, and this is all that he loses.

12.28

In response to those who ask: "Where do you see the gods, or from what source do you perceive that they exist, so that you worship them thus?" I answer, first, that they are visible even with the eyes (in the form of the heavenly bodies). Second, I have never seen my soul, yet I honor it. So too with the gods, whose power affects me daily. From all this, I know that they exist, and therefore I am reverent.

12.29

The salvation of human life is in this: seeing what each thing is in its entirety, both its material and its cause; also in performing just actions and speaking the truth with one's entire soul. What is left but to enjoy the benefits of such a life, joining one good action to another without leaving the smallest interval between them?

12.31

What do you seek? To continue existing? To enjoy your perceptions and your impulses? To swell up and then to shrink back down again? To use your voice and your thoughts? Which of these do you suppose to be worthy of your longing? But if you do well to despise all of these, then follow Reason and the god all the way to the end. But he battles the god and Reason who honors these other things and is distressed because death will take them away.

12.32

How small a portion of the infinite and gaping abyss of time has been assigned to each person! For it soon disappears into eternity. And how small a portion of the whole of being, of the Universal Soul. On what a small piece of earth you creep. Once you have pondered this, do not imagine anything to be of any magnitude, except acting as your nature guides you and enduring whatever Universal Nature may bring.

Glossary of Key Terms and Concepts

ART. See CRAFT.

AXIOM. See PRINCIPLE.

CARE (*therapeia*). Also translated as "tending" or "service." This is the root of the English word "therapy," and it reminds us that philosophy from the beginning was seen as a kind of healing through the redirection of one's attention to the SOUL. (1.7; 2.13; 3.13; Greek synonyms for *therapeia*: 2.5; 6.10,16; 8.8; 12.3)

CONTEMPLATION (*theorein*). This is the origin of the English words "theory," "theoretical," as well as related terms. This was viewed by many ancient philosophers as the highest and most abstract function of the INTELLIGENCE. (1.7; 3.2; 10.11)

COSMOS (*kosmos*). Also translated as "universe," this word refers not only to the spatial magnitude but also to the beauty and order of the entire universe. Marcus Aurelius sometimes uses the word "Whole" (*holos*) as a synonym. The beauty and order of the cosmos come from the REASON or order (*logos*) which governs it. (4.23,27; 6.38; *holos* 2.9; 10.6; 12.26)

CRAFT (*technê*). Also translated as "skill" or "art," this is the root for the English "technical." It refers to what we would call the arts as well as various skills or crafts. The Greeks and Romans did not distinguish between the art of carpentry, for example, and a "fine art" like sculpture or painting. Some have translated this word as "know-how." (4.20,31; 6.16,35; 11.5)

DIVINE SPIRIT. See SPIRIT.

EMOTION (*pathos*). The English word is derived from Greek and Latin words meaning "to move." Therefore, emotions have been conceived of as things which move us and are somewhat out of our control. The task of philosophy, then, is to train our emotional reactions so that we are not ruled by these "movers." (1.9; 3.4; 6.51)

ERROR (*hamartia*). This concept is also translated in this book as "mistake" and "go astray." Both the related noun and verb originally expressed the idea of missing a target. *Hamartia* is used in the New Testament and has commonly been translated by the English word "sin." *Hamartia* is also the word that Aristotle used in the *Poetics*, which we know as "tragic flaw." (1.10; 2.1; 6.27; 9.42; 10.30; 11.18; 12.26)

EXCELLENCE (*aretê*). Most translators have carried over the Latin equivalent *virtus* into the English "virtue." But that word has too much of a strictly moral connotation. We must remember that even well into the philosophical age, the Greek word retained its original functional meaning. A chair possesses *aretê* when it is well built, thus performing its function well. This word applies to humans in the same manner. Therefore, we possess *aretê* when we are living up to our human and moral potential, for which we were made. (2.13; 3.7; 6.48; 9.16)

FREEDOM. See INDEPENDENCE.

GOD/GODS (*theos*). Also translated as "the divine." Many translators of the nineteenth and early twentieth centuries translated this word as "God," for they saw it as parallel to the Christian God. We must keep in mind, however, that Greek and Roman philosophers, and Stoics in particular, were generally opposed to viewing the gods as personifications, and rather understood a god as a governing and ordering principle of the cosmos. We have retained the word "god," but with a lowercase "g" so as to avoid confusion with its Judeo-Christian counterpart. (1.17; 2.4; 5.27; 6.7,44; gods and prayer 9.40; existence of the gods 12.28)

GODLIKE (*theoeidês*). Closely related to the notion of acting in accordance with NATURE, the Stoic ideal is to live a life which is closest to that of the gods. This notion is based on the idea that we all have a divine "spark" inside us, which gives us all superhuman, or divine potential. To be *merely* human is to deny the divine part of ourselves, whereas to tend and cultivate the divine element of ourselves is to be *truly* human. This theory is most likely influenced by Plato, who says in his dialogue *Theaetetus* that the best way of life is to be as godlike as possible. (2.5; 5.34; 6.35)

GUIDING-PART, GOVERNING PART (*hêgêmonikon*). Also "ruling part." The Greek and Roman philosophers viewed the human soul as composed of parts, or aspects, which can be either in harmony or in conflict with each other. Right ordering consists in allowing the naturally rational part to control the lower appetitive parts, with the result being a *harmonia* of the entire person. Vice and unhappiness result from a kind of inner mutiny, in which the lower appetitive parts rule over the rational, and the latter works in the service of the former. (3.4,5; 4.39; 5.3,11,27; 6.8,36; 7.55; 8.48; 11.18; 12.1; as internal god 3.5). See PRINCIPLE for the concept of a guiding principle.

IMPRESSION, IMAGINING (*phantasia*). Also translated as "thought" in a general sense or "conception." An impression is anything which is "impressed" on our minds, either from external sense phenomena or internally from EMOTIONS, thoughts, or internal sensations. For the Stoics, this is the necessary first step in the cognitive process, and right living lies not in the character of these impressions but in our reactions to them. The task of philosophy, then, is to master one's reactions to such impressions through study and meditation. (1.17; 3.4,6,11; 4.24; 5.2,16; 6.16; 8.26,29,49)

INDEPENDENCE (*eleutheria*). This word is often translated as "freedom." For Marcus Aurelius, the word refers primarily to a state of inner freedom, rather than freedom from external constraints, which are often beyond one's control. (2.5; 4.3; 6.16; 8.48)

INTELLIGENCE (*nous*). Also translated as "mind" or "Mind." This is the highest and most rational part of the SOUL and is the faculty by which we can perceive and understand the world at its most real and most good. (2.1,12; 3.7; 5.27, 30; 6.40, 51; 9.9)

JUDGMENT (*hupolêpsis*). Also "grasp," "decision," or "choice." This is the faculty by which we perceive and assess the IMPRESSIONS which affect the SOUL. (3.9; 4.3,11,37; 9.13, 32; 11.11,18; 12.22)

JUSTICE (*dikê, dikaiosunê*). Some have translated this word as "morality," but this captures only part of the word's applications. "Justice" remains the best English word, for it is a concept which has its roots in legal terminology but applies to every aspect of our behavior toward others and ourselves. Plato, in *The Republic*, defines justice internally as a right ordering of the parts of the SOUL and externally as the right ordering of the parts of a society. (1.14; 2.5; 3.6; 5.33; 9.4; 10.11; 11.1; 12.1; same as wisdom 4.37)

LEISURE (*scholê*). Also translated as "rest" or "relief." This is the source of the English word "school," and so we must assume it is not the same as idleness. On the contrary, for the Greek and Roman philosophers, it is idleness which motivates people to be busybodies and workaholics. Leisure, on the other hand, is the environment and state of mind in which one is relatively free from manual labor and concerns of survival, which only then allows time for study and meditation. (4.18,24; 6.7)

MIND. See INTELLIGENCE.

NATURE (*phusis*). The origin of the English "physics" and "physical." In English, we have two senses of the word: nature as in "the beauty of nature," meaning the outdoors, and nature as in "it is his nature to do that" or "he's a natural." The former notion gets its name from being a product of the latter, which refers to the innermost being of a thing, or "what it is," and also its function. Nature with a capital "N" is the force which is behind all things that grow, and this is apparent from the origin of the Greek verb *phuein,* which means "to grow." It is also referred to by Marcus as Universal Nature. (1.9; 2.1; 4.49; 5.1,3,8; 6.33; 7.55; 9.3,42)

PHILOSOPHY (*philosophia*). Love or pursuit of wisdom. See introduction for a discussion of Marcus' conception of philosophy. (1.6; 2.17; 5.9)

PRINCIPLE (*dogma*). Also translated as "guiding-principle," "life-principle," or "rules of living." This word, which has been transliterated into English as "dogma," has not been a popular word in recent times. For the Greeks, (and many Christians) however, it is not a rigid law to be accepted and followed blindly. Rather, a *dogma* is a concept which is meant to be meditated upon and realized or actualized in one's life, the value of which is learned through experience and adherence. (3.10,13; 4.3; 5.9; 6.35; 10.34; 11.5,18)

REGRET, REMORSE (*metanoia*). This is the same word as in the New Testament and is translated as "repentance." In general, it implies a change of mind but also a deep dissatisfaction with one's previous decisions or actions. (8.2, 10, 53)

REASON (*logos*). Translated as "word" in the opening sentence of the Gospel of John: "In the beginning was the word." While *logos* can mean reason, cause, discourse, or conversation, in the *Meditations* it often refers to the principle which orders all things in the COSMOS, and will sometimes be translated with a capital "R." In the context of philosophical discourse, it is used to signify both the form and the content of what is being said. In an individual, reason is what INTELLIGENCE uses in order to make a right decision. (2.5; 3.4,6; 4.4,29,30; 5.27; 9.10,42; 12.31; shared with the gods 6.35)

SKILL. See CRAFT.

SOUL (*psuchê*). The root for our word "psyche" in "psychology." In Greek thought, the *psuchê* is generally thought to be what animates all living creatures ("animate" is from Latin, meaning "things which have an *anima*, or soul"). This higher part is all that remains of our essential humanity. (4.3; 5.11; 7.55; 8.51; 12.28,32; reasoning soul 6.14; 7.55; 9.8; 11.1)

SPIRIT (*daimon*). Also "divine spirit." This is the origin of the English word "demon," but here it does not yet have a purely negative association. For the Greeks, a *daimon* is a lower class of deity, which could enter (or possess) a person. The most famous *daimon* of Greek philosophy is that of Socrates. In the *Apology*, Socrates says that his *daimon* is a sort of inner guide, which tells him only when he is not doing what he ought to. For the Stoics, it also serves as an internal guide, to whom we refuse to listen at our peril. In the *Symposium*, Plato describes Eros, the god of love, as a *daimon* because he is an intermediary between humans and gods. The Christian concept of spirit (especially the Holy Spirit) comes from a different Greek term, *pneuma,* which is associated with breath. (2.13, 17; 5.27; 6.38; 8.45; the god within 3.5)

TENDING. See CARE.

UNIVERSAL NATURE. See NATURE.

UNIVERSE. See COSMOS.

WHOLE. See COSMOS.

Further Reading

For those who are interested in continuing their study of Marcus Aurelius and his thought, we have included a brief list of works which have been of help to us in our effort.

Other writings of Marcus Aurelius

C. R. Haines (editor), The *Correspondence of Marcus Cornelius Fronto*. Loeb Classical Library, 1920 and later reprintings.

An important—and much neglected—companion to the *Meditations*, for it serves to bring out the human side of the emperor through these intimate and touching letters to a contemporary. As we read the emperor's letters, it becomes clear that our understanding of Marcus Aurelius the man must be taken within the different contexts of his intended audience, be it himself (*Meditations*) or a dear friend and mentor

(Fronto). As a result, we see two very different *personae* which nevertheless belong to the same person.

Translations

George Long, *The Meditations of Marcus Aurelius.* Shambhala Press, 1993 reprint.

This late-nineteenth-century translation was intended for the general reader and has inspired generations of readers because of its accessibility and readability.

Maxwell Staniforth, *The Meditations of Marcus Aurelius.* Penguin, 1964 and reprinted.

While Staniforth has taken many liberties with the Greek text, he often more closely approaches the meaning of the original than more literal translations do. Extremely useful by itself or as a companion to a more literal translation.

G. M. A. Grube, *Marcus Aurelius: The Meditations.* Library of Liberal Arts, 1963 and later reprintings.

Grube produced an accurate and readable translation for those who are perhaps more academically inclined.

Books on Marcus Aurelius and Stoicism

Pierre Hadot, *The Inner Citadel.* Translated by Michael Chase. Harvard University Press, 1998.

Hadot is one of the few scholars whose work on the ancient philosophers emphasizes the ancient concept of philosophy as a way of life. This book is a study of the philosophy of the *Meditations*, and Marcus' philosophical influences, all from this very practical perspective on philosophy. For an example of Hadot's approach to ancient philosophy in general, also see his *What Is Ancient Philosophy?* (Harvard University Press, 2002).

Anthony Birley, *Marcus Aurelius.* Routledge, 2000 reprint.

This book looks at Marcus' life and thought from a historical and political perspective and shows us the environment in which Marcus struggled to stay true to his philosophical ideals.

A. A. Long, *Hellenistic Philosophy.* University of California Press, 1986 reprint.

This is the standard introduction to Stoicism and its major exponents, as well as to the contemporary schools of Epicureanism and Skepticism. Long's *Epictetus* (Oxford, 2002) also sheds much light on the philosophical and literary influences on the *Meditations*.

R. B. Rutherford, *The Meditations of Marcus Aurelius: A Study.* Oxford University Press, 1989 and 2000 reprint.

Rutherford sees Marcus' literary style as an important and much-neglected component in our understanding of the *Meditations* as a whole.

Greek Text

In our translation, we have made use of the revised edition of Joachim Dalfen (Teubner, Leipzig, 1987), as well as the text, translation, and commentary of A. S. L. Farquharson (Oxford, 1944). Our primary resource for translating Book One has been the critical edition, with French translation and commentary by Pierre Hadot (Paris, Bude series, Les Belles Lettres, 1998). This is the first of a multi-volume series covering the entire *Meditations*, and we anxiously await future volumes. The extremely literal Latin translation of J. M. Schultz (1802) was also of much help. Our choice of readings was determined more by comprehensibility than scholarly textual disputes. For the most part, we have used the commonly accepted readings, unless an interpolation simply made more sense to us and added to the comprehensibility of the text.

About the Translators

The author of *Why Can't We Be Good?*, *The American Soul*, and *The Heart of Philosophy*, **Jacob Needleman** is professor of philosophy at San Francisco State University, and former Director of the Center for the Study of New Religions at the Graduate Theological Union, Berkeley. He was educated at Harvard, Yale, and the University of Freiburg, Germany, and has also served as a research associate at the Rockefeller Institute for Medical Research and was a research fellow at Union Theological Seminary. He lives in Oakland, California.

John P. Piazza has earned degrees in philosophy and religion and in classics. He has taught philosophy, Latin, ancient Greek, and religion at the high school and college levels. He currently teaches at St. Vincent de Paul High School in Petaluma, California.

Accept This Gift
Selections from *A Course in Miracles*
Edited by Frances Vaughan, Ph.D., and Roger Walsh, M.D., Ph.D.
Foreword by Marianne Williamson

"An invaluable collection from one of the great sources of the perennial wisdom—a gold mine of psychological and spiritual insights."

—KEN WILBER

January 2008   ISBN 978-1-58542-619-5

The Kybalion
Three Initiates

Who wrote this mysterious guide to the principles of esoteric psychology and worldly success? History has kept readers guessing. . . . Experience for yourself the intriguing ideas of an underground classic.

May 2008   ISBN 978-1-58542-643-0

The Spiritual Emerson
Ralph Waldo Emerson, introduction by Jacob Needleman

This concise volume collects the core writings that have made Ralph Waldo Emerson a key source of insight for spiritual seekers of every faith—with an introduction by the bestselling philosopher Jacob Needleman.

July 2008   ISBN 978-1-58542-642-3